Tellwell Talent
www.tellwell.ca

ISBN
978-1-77302-767-8 (Hardcover)
978-1-77302-771-5 (Paperback)
978-1-77302-769-2 (eBook)

Magician to Mystic

A Mediumistic Path to a Spiritual Life

Brian Robertson and Simon James

Dedication

We dedicate this book to the family
to which we belong...

Acknowledgements

We gratefully acknowledge the literary assistance of
Debra Skelton and the generous support of Terri Woolgar,
Deborah Davis, Anne Welch, Lorna Lyons and Beverley Stokes.

Brian Robertson & Simon James

Brian Robertson and Simon James are internationally recognised experts in their field. They travel the world as renowned exponents of a classical oral tradition of esoteric mediumship and offer an understanding of its ancient foundations to a new generation of spiritual seekers. They work with health professionals, artists, psychologists, educators, craftspeople and individuals from almost every discipline, fostering the innate ability to tap into that wealth of inspiration open to us all, and which they call "everyday mediumship".

Robertson and James have shared the breadth of their unique knowledge in documentary film and television, and as guest lecturers on international podiums worldwide. They are directors of the Inner Quest in Victoria, Canada where they offer a curriculum of classical study for the ethical development of the medium and the serious student of the intuitive arts.

Foreword

Thousands of years ago, our ancestors drew imagery in the dark caves seeking union with the hidden, mysterious aspects of being.

Centuries later, others created sacred writing, incantations which they inscribed on cuneiform tablets and carved in hieroglyphs upon temple walls, elaborate pyramids, tombs and sarcophagi. They filled papyrus rolls with magical spells, calling one into the realms beyond the seen. The middle ages birthed grimoires which continued to explore the magic of being.

Yet, with the arrival of the Age of Reason, humanity's focus turned away from the mystical. Thankfully all that is about to change with the appearance of this book, *Magician to Mystic*.

Beautifully written, its mystics, Simon James and Brian Robertson, reopen the doors to explore the hidden realms sourced through true devotion. They give us a treasure, a book for all seekers of Truth, shining a light on the pathway to understanding. They move us beyond the smoke and mirrors of waking perception to the reality of the spiritual connection that rests in the heart of all Creation.

Robertson and James open wide the portal to all who authentically wish to move within in search of the dwelling place of the Eternal, the hidden origin and source of our being. Their presence emanates from each page, creating a joyful and true guide to all pilgrims of the Way. I predict it shall be cherished, and consulted over and again!

Janet Piedilato, PhD
Author of *Pieda's Tales*
Creator of the *Mystical Dream Tarot*

Table of Contents

Chapter Five: Spirituality and Mediumship   51

Chapter Six: Nature of the Intuitive Arts   61

Chapter Seven: Quality of Discernment   75

Chapter Eight: Becoming a Balanced Medium   87

Yggdrasil

"An ash I know, there stands,
Yggdrasil is its name,
A tall tree, showered
with shining loam.
From there come the dews that drop in the valleys.
It stands forever green over
Urðr's well."

The cosmic tree of life is a significant symbol in almost every culture. It speaks of circular time, of the continuous regeneration of all life, and of immortality. It dwells in the many worlds, connecting heaven, earth and the underworld. It gives succour and spiritual wisdom. The tree embodies the mystic's journey. To the magician, it represents the desire of belief; to the medium, it is an invisible icon; to the mystic, it is Creation, Life itself.

Let us begin …

Introduction

*"Think only on those things that are in line with your principles
and can bear the light of day."*

Heraclitus[1]

This book speaks to the spiritual seeker, to the one who is searching for a pathway to a spiritual life. Whether you are a working medium, a novice, or someone who simply wishes to understand, you are invited to explore the elements of the medium's art in pursuit of that most human of aspirations: to unfold a path of spiritual progression.

Within these pages you shall discover the principles of mediumship, their link to ancient wisdom and their connection to Natural Law. As we climb a ladder of light intended to lead us toward knowledge of the mysteries, may you discover the riches that lie upon your personal pathway to God through the medium's way. May this book shed some light upon your own inner quest.

Brian Robertson and Simon James are internationally recognised experts in their field. They travel the world as renowned exponents of a classical oral tradition of esoteric mediumship rooted in ancient knowledge, and offer an understanding of its foundations to a new generation of seekers within the spiritual experience.

The rare knowledge they possess is sadly in danger of being diluted and unwittingly distorted by the passing spiritual trends of the day and age. Consequently, their students and peers worldwide have long urged them to share their profound understanding of mediumship and its ancient mystical principles as a dynamic way of life for the modern world. "Sooner rather than later" has been the common cry; hence this book.

Although a great deal has been written about mediumship, spirituality and mysticism, much of the existing literature of the past is either outdated in its references or written in a style which the modern mind finds difficult to comprehend. Today, on the other hand, we often see hastily assembled partial truths offered in digestible bites for the quick gratification of the spiritual appetite.

For this reason, Brian Robertson and Simon James offer the spiritual seeker a modern, down-to-earth perspective on the vital nature of mediumship as a pathway to a spiritual life in the 21ˢᵗ century. They take you back to the foundations of mediumistic and esoteric spirituality, to its truths.

Over the period of many years, Robertson and James have created a rich curriculum of classical study which lays the foundation for the healthy and well-rounded development of the medium. They have revitalised ancient knowledge, knowledge which has everything to do with the sacred art of mediumship but which was at risk of vanishing from view altogether.

Thanks to the work of these two remarkable teachers, our generation may once again tap into the deep reservoir of wisdom evoked by the Triads and the Archetypes, as was practised within our tradition. Aspects of these teachings are now being assimilated and shared by other practitioners and teachers around the world.

They sincerely hope that *Magician to Mystic* will nurture all who wish to understand more about the nature of mediumship, mysticism, and its spiritual roots. In so doing, they also hope to do away with the many outlandish misconceptions around mediumistic practice and bring its inherent naturalness into the light of day.

Joseph Campbell once said that myths are the "Literature of the Spirit."[2] They shine a light on the spiritual potential within every human being. The myths which have been selected speak to the soul with messages of wisdom, and in such a way as to rekindle that state of awe in which our souls thrive and breathe, and without which we cannot truly be aware of the presence of the Spirit.

Brian Robertson and Simon James trust that the riches contained in this book may awaken your curiosity and touch your heart.

If you are reading these words, it is possible that your soul may be ready to look more deeply than before at the nature of your life, and your mind and heart be willing to open to those truths which your spirit already knows.

Debra Skelton

The Sorcerer's Apprentice

There was once a great sorcerer renowned for his wisdom and knowledge. Long years of study had given him mastery of nature and many things would come to life at his word.

One day, leaving home to travel, he charged his apprentice with the cleaning of his home. When the sorcerer had gone, the apprentice knew what he would do. The house was far too big to clean by himself so he would use magic. Uttering the words he had heard the sorcerer use, a mop immediately came to life and began to carry buckets of water to clean the floor. The apprentice was pleased at first, until he saw a flood rising inside the house. In panic, he tried every incantation he could recall, but all in vain and now he was fearful of drowning.

Suddenly, the water vanished and everything returned to normal. There stood the sorcerer, returned home. The apprentice feared punishment but the sorcerer knew that the apprentice had already learned his lesson. True knowledge and wisdom come only through study and hard work.

Ignorance

Chapter One:
A Message from Simon and Brian

Enlightenment

Enlightenment is a concept found in almost every great religious philosophy. It describes the action of seeking spiritual insight which, in our tradition, must include the return to our true nature, which is the Divine within.

As long as we believe that enlightenment is to be found outside of ourselves, we miss the point. Sometimes, in the well-meaning pursuit of our enlightenment, there is a tendency to go spiritual shopping, to grasp at this method or to try on that philosophy. As a result we may well undergo a series of so-called "revelations" that are masked in the outer garments of a feel-good philosophy. But outer garments eventually wear thin.

It is no wonder that we seek spiritual footholds outside of ourselves, living as we do in a culture which rarely encourages the natural faculty of intuition or inner contemplation. Instead, we create heroes, follow mentors, and idolise Hollywood stars because we fail to recognise the greatness within ourselves. We become focused on distractions rather than being.

Intuition of the soul creates peace. However, modern society doesn't teach us intuition. Society teaches us to create patterns. In school, we learn quickly which sequence of actions results in a top grade on the report card; in business, which approach will get us the job; in the home, what a good parent should look like. Our society doesn't always celebrate the development of intuitive talents, of excellence in art, music, mathematics, plumbing, baking, caregiving, or fulfilling our creative natures – those talents which are uniquely ours.

In our tradition, we nurture the intuitive nature, the natural inner knowing that leads us back to our Beauty. For us, these are the very foundations, the bricks under our feet as we unfold upon the path of enlightenment. We are called to embrace our own power, that which has been divinely bestowed upon us. Until we understand that, and act upon it, we will not create a peaceful life.

Enlightenment is not just about sitting and bathing in the light, becoming one with everything. We must act. We must do. We must feel. Then we may come to know. We can have many enlightenments in a lifetime, not just one all-consuming, "I get it." It is a matter of many life experiences, not just one event.

The Mystical Nature

In an age of sensory bombardment, it is hardly surprising that our innate sense of awe is drowned out almost from birth. Sadly, that natural sense of devotion has, for many of us, gone completely underground.

But without a sense of wonder, how can we hope to recognise the magnitude of the spirit when we touch it? Until we can feel reverence, how shall we be aware of the presence of the One?

Awe is the receptive sense of our soul, as are the fingertips to physical touch. Neither the mind nor the heart has sufficiently subtle means to fully discern the essence of spirit. This does not mean that we lay reason aside. It simply means that we explore another experience of perception. It invites us to be vulnerable, not foolish.

As we begin to rekindle the feelings of wonderment and reverence that were once so natural to us as children, we re-open the possibility of developing our mystical eyes and ears using reason as our silent companion.

As traditional religions loosen their grip on societies all over the western world, people are discovering that, while the mind is freer to think for itself, it often leaves them in a quandary. Where to turn? What philosophy speaks to me? For the soul must have sustenance and so it seeks another kind of spiritual footing.

Consequently, we often see westerners looking to other cultures for spiritual nourishment. More often than not, they turn to eastern philosophies seeking divine knowledge and the mystical experience for which the soul yearns. Indeed, there are great spiritual riches to be found there.

But westerners are a heart-centred culture. To submit such a nature to mind-centred disciplines is to diminish, if not destroy, the mediumistic ability of a westerner, just as to submit the eastern mind to a heart-centred culture can create chaos in the psyche. We cannot plant a cactus in a rainforest or bluebells in a desert and expect a good result. Even when we share core beliefs, which we most certainly do, mixing practices is an error of judgment, especially for those on the mediumistic path.

That said, our theurgic tradition shares a great many central truths with mystical traditions from cultures around the world. Throughout these pages, we acknowledge not only figures within our own lineage, but also those from other lineages whose words echo the sacred knowledge held within all great mystical traditions.

Dispelling Myths About Mediumship

Inspiration is the birthright of all human beings. The spiritual current that moves the inspired medium is the same current that has moved countless others in all areas of human endeavour, and in all cultures.

In this book, we address what is commonly called mediumship, dispelling some outdated misconceptions and revitalising an awareness of the inherent spiritual nature of the art of mediumship itself. We speak directly to working mediums who seek more depth and meaning in their work, as well as to sensate individuals who simply wish to bring a quality of genuine, natural spirituality back into their everyday lives. We speak to all who seek the presence of the power of the Spirit in their life and in their work.

And to all, we say again and again that the real reason for communication with the physically "dead" is not to prove that there is life after death, but that there is life before death. The common message contained within all mediumistic communication is this: live your life to its fullest in the here and now, within your true nature, and be awake to the freedom of experience that is yours both in this life and in the afterlife. For it is but one continuous Life.

For the first time outside of our classroom, we publicly introduce some of the concepts that have long preoccupied us as exponents of the sacred art of mediumship, or transcommunication. Here, for example, we touch upon just a few of the many Triads which we have coalesced over time as a foundation for the unfoldment of a truly healthy medium. We also share some facets of our original work with the archetypes within the mediumistic tradition, as we have developed and integrated them for the emerging medium.

Above all, we wish to broaden that threadbare notion of mediumship as an exclusive talent possessed by a gifted few who deliver messages from the spirit world. It is perhaps time to bring common sense and light to this definition, and to speak of inspiration before we speak of mediumship.

Inspiration, in Middle English, means *divine guidance*. All human beings have the potential to be both the inspired and the inspirer because we are all connected to the Soul of All. How we receive that inspiration, the patterns it forms within our minds, and then how we express it outwardly depends upon our individual natures which, all being unique, have resulted in an infinite variety of creations throughout human history. Practical inventions, works of art, mathematical theories, musical compositions and medical discoveries – in short, *everything* we have ever created is the outflowing of inspiration. We all become the medium for inspired thought and, in this sense, we become an everyday medium.

A medium is one who listens. This ability lies within each of us as we open ourselves to listen to the inspiration of our soul. It has nothing to do with our religious beliefs or philosophical outlook, nor is it the exclusive domain of the so-called spiritually advanced. The ability is inherent within our very makeup as human beings.

The way we choose to manifest the inspired ideas we receive is our talent. A surgeon may receive an insight into a lifesaving procedure; the writer, a vision of a particular character; or a parent, a creative way to help a child overcome a learning disability. All people are natural mediums of creative thought, though some choose to listen more closely than others.

As the 19th century French philosopher, Edouard Schuré said, "For how can we imagine a thinker, a poet, an inventor, a hero, a master of science or of art, a genius of any kind, without a mighty ray of those two master-faculties which make the mystic and the occultist – the inner vision and the sovereign intuition."[1]

Inspiration is natural. Mediumship is natural. However, the individual we call a medium who has the ability to receive inspiration and communication from a discarnate source practises a highly specialised art. In this sense, mediums are born, not made, and face many unusual challenges that come with their ability, some of which we shall address in this volume.

It is our hope that, within these pages, we may reinvigorate the spiritual essence of the art of transcommunication for those who practise it, and that we may offer encouragement to all who read this book, whatever your chosen path, as you move toward unfolding your true nature. For in revealing your nature you open yourselves up to the soul's inspiration.

For we say to you that no one needs fixing, because no one is broken. We need only find our right balance. When we are in balance, we are in our peace. The world may say that you need this to be happy, that to be successful, or this to be fulfilled. No. Just find the contentment that comes from being in your nature.

When you awaken to who you are, to your true nature, then you may truly begin on the path of enlightenment. As you discover the beauty within, you begin to create the beauty without. The beauty that comes from healing.

And, whether or not you practise what we call the art of mediumship, know that the power of the Spirit has a place within your soul to create its own unique and magnificent vision.

> *"May you blossom well without judgment or fear,*
> *so that others may gaze upon your Beauty."*

Brian Robertson and Simon James

The Heart of Your Ability

You are the guardian of your own talent. Protect it, nurture it and treat it respectfully. So too, understand that the holistic development of your psychic ability is the selfsame thing as the realisation of your true nature. Your true nature is a facet of the Divine, and the very heart of the temple within.

May we take this moment to offer a word of advice to all of you who are courageous enough to tread this path from Magician to Mystic.

In the beginning stages of development, students pass through the infant consciousness of the magician, which we shall speak about later. Once some basic skills have been acquired, students of mediumship sometimes find themselves confronted by the very real temptations of the cult of celebrity which unfortunately pervade the world of mediumship.

In eastern philosophy, they speak of the siddhis, those psychic abilities which occur after a lifetime of spiritual unfoldment through practices such as meditation and yoga. Spiritual enlightenment comes first, and phenomena may follow as a secondary reflection of their advancement.

In the western world, however, a curious craving for all manner of psychic phenomena often seems to be the primary goal. Psychic manifestation, in and of itself, becomes the ultimate prize. The soul progression of the practitioner, having therefore no causal link to the phenomena, will not necessarily follow.

Without a spiritual foothold, some individuals choose to take the path of least resistance when faced with the pressure-cooker of public expectation. Consciously or not, they masquerade their psychic abilities in the guise of mediumship, dazzling us with quantities of psychic data; the illusion creates an assumption that it is received from a loved one, or a higher intelligence. This is not only damaging to their own talent but deprives the recipients of a healing experience.

Remember, mediumship is the demonstration of living consciousness. It is about Intelligence, not data. Anything less should not be called mediumship.

Sadly, during the course of our careers, we have seen many promising mediums utterly mesmerised by the allure of fame and influence over others. We have seen the fullness of their potential irreparably diminished as they resort to protecting their ego at all costs. If you yourself recognise that the comforts of notoriety are what give you satisfaction, we urge you to be honest about that - and then put this book down. It is not for you.

For others, we strongly encourage you to investigate the nature of your training and seek out teachers who hold the knowledge that will guide your soul and your ability to their shining point.

Do not be shy about asking your teachers where they were taught, or who their own teachers were. If you have studied concepts such as the Triads, the Archetypes or Sitting in the Presence, for instance, these have likely been passed down to you, hopefully with our permission, by our own students. Ask them how long they have worked with their ability before they began teaching. Ask them if they themselves sit in the Presence, what role self-healing played in their development and what their spiritual foundations are.

Seek only the best for your talent and for your soul illumination. Would you not do as much for a precious child of yours?

Know the lineage of your teachers. The heart of your ability is in your own hands.

The Prince and the Sphinx

There was once a prince of Egypt called Thutmose. He was the favoured son of the Pharaoh, and so his jealous brothers plotted against him. Thutmose became troubled and escaped frequently into the desert. One day, his attention was caught by the colossal carving of the Sphinx, spirit of Harmachis, god of the rising sun. After many centuries it lay half-buried in the sand. Resting between its paws, Thutmose fell into a dream-filled sleep. Harmachis spoke to him saying, "Look upon me and know that the sand covers me. Reveal me once again and you will sit upon the throne of Egypt. Do this and the Lands shall be yours. Draw near to me and I will always be with you."

Upon waking, Thutmose returned to court and ordered the Sphinx to be uncovered. Within the year, his brothers proclaimed him heir to the throne. Thutmose became one of the greatest pharaohs of Egypt.

Destiny

Chapter Two:
Magician to Mystic

"When you allow yourself to go from eagerness to reason, mechanics to meaning, then you begin the pathway of the mystic."

Brian Robertson

Everyday Mediumship

Mediums can be found in all walks of life. Whether a person is religious, atheist, spiritually aware or not, mediums can be seen working in all fields of human endeavour; in the arts, sciences, politics, academia, in the workforce and in family life. However, you will not find these individuals demonstrating mediumship on a public platform, doing psychic readings or giving private sittings. In fact, they have nothing whatsoever to do with those professions normally associated with the intuitive arts.

And yet, we have had the privilege of training and working with these individuals extensively over the years, with those who have sought the unfoldment of their natural faculties to be used in whichever way their soul's calling demands. They seek the art of the mystery in the quest for healing, inspiration and wisdom. They take the understanding of our oral tradition and our teachings, and use it in their chosen professions of medicine, business, family life, corporate coaching, counselling, the arts and even within other religious disciplines.

For such sensate individuals, as well as for professional practitioners of the intuitive arts, we trust that *Magician to Mystic* will clarify the oral tradition in which we work and offer an understanding of the spirituality that underlies this tradition, a tradition that is meaningful to all who seek a spiritual foundation in their lives.

We offer an awakening. An awakening to the magic of being alive, to the sacredness of all life and our oneness with the God of Our Own Understanding. An awakening to the knowledge that spirit and matter are not separate. An awakening to the truth that authentic spirituality is simply one's own honesty, morality and integrity. We become...

> *Awake to the Outer World.* Attuning through observation to the natural cycles of nature and harmonising our rhythms with those of the seasons; attuning to the unity with the spirit of all things and to the sense of community with all life.

> *Awake to the Inner World.* Committing to an inner discipleship of contemplation and practice in which we develop our creative talents, intellectual potential, compassionate humanity and spiritual understanding, and embrace the holistic use of spiritual and physical methods to promote health and longevity.

> *Awake to the Upper World.* Allowing the deepening awareness of worlds within worlds, of our ancestors, and of other realities verified by certain disciplines within our tradition.

And so we speak to all who seek an insight into the jewelled facets of life, who seek to celebrate life by embracing the truth of Self, and thereby embracing the wisdom of the Creator.

The Intuitive Arts

In our lifetime's experience as mediums and teachers, we have encountered again and again some basic questions regarding mediumship, psychism, mysticism and the many related avenues of practice. We have remarked that there are often some lapses in spiritual and technical understanding, not only amongst our students but occasionally amongst some practising professionals. We sincerely hope to bring a fuller perspective and some clarification to these often misunderstood, but profoundly magnificent subjects. Within these pages, we speak not only to the practising intuitive but to all who sincerely seek a foundation of spiritual understanding in their daily lives.

Let us begin by saying that all facets of the intuitive arts are actually aspects of a whole, rooted in the Divine Mind. This must be the foundation of our understanding. The faculty of mediumship is just that, a faculty. It is not in itself a pathway to the Divine, for until we understand its inherently devotional purpose, which is that of healing, it remains merely a mechanical activity.

All things originate with Spirit, and therefore all areas of practice are related expressions of its manifestation. In our view, in our belief, and in our certain knowledge, the practice of transcommunication is a sacred art. We must be aware that it is a privileged means of service to the spirit world, and an outflowing expression of the Great Spirit or God of Your Own Understanding.

Without this recognition of the source and the purpose of our ability, mediumship divorces itself from its mystical foundations and becomes a hollow, purely mechanical practice which, in time, may well take a personal toll on practitioner and recipient alike.

Within mediumship today, many practitioners are engrossed in the practical execution of their craft and may dismiss esoteric knowledge of their art as being of little worth or even a waste of time. They may choose to remain in what we call the magician consciousness. However, practice without training, training without knowledge, and knowledge without wisdom prove untrustworthy when faced with our greatest human challenges.

In our tradition we distinguish between knowledge and practice. Those who aspire to the mystic consciousness must have both. For knowledge will ultimately illumine one's practice and practice will corroborate one's knowledge.

One of the great philosophers of our lineage, Plotinus, once said, "The goal of philosophy is to awaken individuals to the reality beyond the material world. But philosophy alone cannot take a person to the highest reality of the One. Only mystical experience can unite an individual with the One."[1]

We, as mediums, are heirs to the theurgic tradition of ancient knowledge. We link, in essence, to that same source of wisdom that has always been there to be discovered by all who earnestly seek it. It is a body of thought and practice which brings the human being, in this case the medium, closer to the divine emanation.

Our tradition is studied as a philosophy and practised as an art. The more deeply we commit to the consciousness of the medium, the greater is our knowing. In our quest, we seek to balance the self in order to become a worthy vessel for the work of the Spirit. The principal challenge lies in this: that we are called to heal. The journey from magician to medium, and from medium to mystic demands that we ourselves come into balance. Inevitably, as we engage in the discipleship, the shadow awakens; meaning that all we may have suppressed, our hidden ambitions, vices or fears, stir and rise again. We then have the free will to confront and heal them, or to suppress once again. We understand the very real causality that exists between the disciplines of personal growth, mechanical development and divine unfoldment.

This is old knowledge. This is our way. These teachings are the very bedrock of the path leading from the mediumistic to the mystic consciousness.

So, with this basic understanding that, as intuitives and mediums, we are all in service to the spirit world first and foremost, we shall now explore the fundamental groundwork of our sensitivity and awareness, throwing light on our approach to the intuitive arts and its inseparable connection to Spirit and spirituality. Within one of the profound ancient texts of our hermetic lineage, *Hymns of Hermes*, we may find encouragement in our spiritual quest: "Understanding is to Comprehend. Wisdom is to see beyond understanding into the God Mind."[2]

Theurgic Mediumship

We belong to a modern mystery school; that is, a body of knowledge, thought and practice in which we draw aside the veil and awaken investigation into the mysteries of spirit, both human and divine. In so doing, we have an opportunity to move from the finite sphere of the magician's art toward the infinite realms of the mystic.

Theurgy or "divine working" finds its known origins in the ancient mystery schools. The purpose is the attainment of spiritual consciousness to bring us to a closer union with the Divine. Theurgical influences are woven throughout history's many religious doctrines, although the mysteries themselves were ever partially hidden from public view within symbol and allegory. These are the common threads of truth we seek in our work as mediums and mystics. These are the mysteries in which we find our shared spiritual heritage and our common humanity, the understanding of which defies any illusion of separation between folk.

Theurgic mediumship is an art which is intentionally cultivated within those sensate individuals who have been born with a mediumistic ability, and who genuinely desire to understand the spiritual substance of their art. During the course of a lengthy discipleship, that natural ability is carefully and spiritually nurtured, finding its illumination as a God-centred art for the good of all living beings.

We seek to reclaim the theurgical foundations of our practice as mediums and as teachers, whose intention it is to guide the serious student through the difficult apprenticeship of the magician, to the expanding awareness of the medium, toward the consciousness of the mystic. As the student moves through his or her apprenticeship, we as educators become facilitators of the mysteries and, in this sense, echo the work of the mystagogues of ancient times.

We have no qualms in stating that this path is not for everyone. The natural law of soul progression is a given for all who will it so, but not every intuitive practitioner is destined to unfold along this particular pathway. Nevertheless, it is our hope that, at the very least, an awareness of the essentially devotional quality of their natural intuitive abilities may somehow colour the way in which they choose to employ them; that is, in service.

Knowledge, as we all know, may be used wisely or foolishly, to build or to destroy. The ignorant wielding of power can be dangerous in the wrong hands. This is equally as true in the material world as in the etheric world. For this reason, the theurgical knowledge that is our heritage is meaningful only to those who understand its purpose as an agent of upliftment to the human soul. It is this intuitive understanding of the ultimate purpose of such knowledge that sparks that unquenchable drive toward theurgical unfoldment within the medium's soul.

Discipleship

In layman's terms, *magic* implies a mastery over the ability to manipulate both the things of this world and the invisible worlds. It is an inner technique with an outer intent, that of controlling the elements of our world. *Mysticism* implies knowledge of hidden divine experience. It is an inner discipline that seeks experience of the divine natural laws underlying all phenomena in the ultimate quest for unity with the One.

In our tradition, the magician's passage is an apprenticeship, a natural stage in which, as the aptitude for mediumship shows itself, one learns the mechanics of the art. It is an apprenticeship of natural magic. In this stage, the components of the magician's skill can be likened in their naturalness to those of the cunning folk of Europe, those folk healers and seers who possessed a native ability to alter their perceptions and thereby alter their reality.

The passage of the magician is a chapter along the way rather than the journey's end. If we become distracted or obsessed by the phenomena and remain in the schoolroom of magic, we lose sight of its purpose and cut short the divine voyage to the mystic. That divine voyage is where the real work of healing begins. Here is where we begin to see divine transformation. Although the mystical experience itself is always a personal one, that experience is then used to create a shift within the collective consciousness. A mystic is there to move, not just the consciousness of one, but the consciousness of the many.

In our tradition, the development of the sensitive from magician to mystic is a discipleship; a commitment not to an individual or a leader or a creed, but to a craft which leads to knowledge of the God Mind. It is our soul's calling that draws us on toward the realisation of our own spirit, through the wondrous and natural mechanics of the magician to the awakened state of the medium, and beyond to the worlds within worlds of the mystic. It is a discipleship along a pathway that leads us toward the Great Spirit, that Divine Intelligence which has many names.

From time to time there seems to be a trend for some students of the intuitive arts to become adherents of a particular medium, more com- mitted to a person and their methods than to the sacred art itself. Some celebrity figures may even offer a certificate of mediumship generally at considerable financial cost to the student. We would caution any serious student of mediumship to remember that the discipleship to which we refer applies to a spiritual pathway, but never to an individual however famous they may be.

We often speak to our students of the need to heal ourselves in order to become fit vessels for the work of the Spirit. This begins with being honest about our motives for wanting to develop our sensitivity. It is of no avail to pursue mediumship as a way of life if your true passion, and therefore your talent, actually lies elsewhere. Our long-term well-being of mind, emotion, and even body, depends upon our truthfulness in this regard.

Do not be tempted by the illusion that there is any kind of automatic spiritual superiority in becoming a medium. Your true spiritual fulfilment lies in the development of your inherent passions and abilities, and not in any false notions fabricated by the child-mind. A truly free will is bound neither by the choices made by ego, nor by the mirage of external success.

The discipleship of the medium also asks that we heal those of our biased patterns and perceptions which interfere with our duty as mediums. We will be touching upon these aspects in later chapters, but for the moment suffice it to say that the serious disciple of the mediumistic path must be prepared to do the considerable work needed to address old patterns in order to uncover their divine nature, their Beauty. Gratitude, a sense of duty, devotion, a desire to serve and inner discipline – these qualities are essential to the development of the mediumistic consciousness. We are speaking of a *mediumistic pathway to a spiritual life.*

This discipleship being understood, our natural forward impetus as developing intuitives will then take us through a series of stages of awareness, or consciousness. Each stage is a natural precursor to the next as we move onward and upward in the fulfilment of our potential as true servants of God. Let us look more closely at each stage.

Consciousness of the Magician

The magician phase of the traditional apprenticeship is where we begin. It is intense, rigorous and lasts for many years. This phase of development is partly a mechanical one through which all developing intuitives must pass. If properly and patiently traversed, however, it lays the solid foundations that uphold the very structure of the medium's practice throughout his or her lifetime. The disciplines established during this time will eventually allow the medium to reach his or her shining point.

During this phase, many levels of skill, knowledge and experience are acquired. An individual begins the journey with healing, development of the self and stimulating the various talents he or she possesses. Technically, the focus is upon honing the individual's ability to receive information beyond that perceived by the five senses, to amplify the inherent psychic faculty and to bring about a recognition of those energies that are, in fact, an extension of psychological and physical processes. Fundamental breathing and visualisation techniques, together with some basic methods which enhance the individual's inherent faculties, all serve to transform the perceptions and awaken the ability of the developing sensitive.

In *Henry IV*, Part I, Shakespeare's character, Glendower boasts, "I can call spirits from the vasty deep" to which Hotspur replies, "Why, so can I, or so can any man; But will they come, when you do call for them?"

The need for a solid foundation of disciplined development cannot be understated. A well-founded medium will have the ability to sustain the mediumistic awareness for a substantial period of time during a demonstration, a discipline which must be strengthened gradually over many years. By the time the medium works professionally, he or she should consistently be able to give a demonstration of between sixty and ninety minutes. The medium who can only sustain one or two contacts with a discarnate communicator has not been adequately trained. Equally, a private sitting should easily last between half an hour and an hour.

Strengthening the qualities of mind, body and emotion in this steady way results in easier access to the intuition, that same intuition which will then inspire and guide the medium indefinitely. It is in the phase of the magician that the individual learns to trust it.

At the same time, the student begins to understand the importance of keeping oral traditions alive and taking personal responsibility for the ethical continuity of this lineage. And so, too, are dawning glimpses of the profound knowledge of the Sacred Power and its monumental significance in the many worlds.

The pitfalls at this stage can be many. "When I was a young student," recalls Simon, "working under Gordon Higginson, I often accompanied him as he demonstrated and lectured across the country. One never knew what to expect or what was going to be asked of us. On this particular occasion, he was to address a group in the library at the Arthur Findlay College in Great Britain. 'Tonight', he said to the full classroom, 'we're going to look at psychometry. And we're going to get Simon and Glyn (Edwards) to demonstrate for you.'

"Well, I'd never done this in public before, *ever!* They went round with a cushion and asked someone to place an object on it so that the person carrying it didn't touch it and I didn't touch it. As I remember, it was a ring. So I psychometrised this ring – and I was *awful!* I was so nervous. It just wasn't good. Then Gordon said, 'Now we'll ask Glyn to do it.' And of course Glyn, who was of a highly dramatic turn, went into every mortal detail and was excellent. Most impressive. I really just wanted to die as I sat there upon the platform. Then at the end, to make things worse, Gordon blithely pronounced, 'Well, ladies and gentlemen, tonight's lesson obviously demonstrates the difference between a developed medium and an undeveloped one!'

"Now, I had two choices. I could either wither under the attack on my pride and go talk to Gordon about it; or I could walk out the door and say, 'Ok, that was an experience. What he said was absolutely true. I don't like it but just get on with it.' Which is what I did.

"Why am I telling you this? Because this is a good example of being within the magician consciousness. There I was, eager to impress, proud to be on a public platform with Glyn Edwards, and acutely aware of being one of only a few private students of the eminent Gordon Higginson. And basically, I crashed to earth!"

In the consciousness of the magician, success depends upon the ability to perform, to produce the goods. The ego is either boosted by public approval or devastated by public humiliation. In the consciousness of the medium, however, our focus begins to turn from self-protection to spiritual service. Failure or success in the public eye is of little matter. Service to the One is. Healing is.

When the ego of the student goes unchecked or when the guidance of the teacher is wanting, we may also at times see psychic demonstrations passed off as communication with the spirit world, frequently in the name of entertainment. Neither is it uncommon, unfortunately, to perpetuate this cycle of weakened magician consciousness by "training" mediums in the space of one to four years. Mediocrity engenders mediocrity. And what began as a mystical spiritual journey can become a circus of entertainment for an unwitting public, a public that mistakenly assumes that performances of such spectacular spirit communication are always a sign of the spiritual advancement of the practitioner.

In the magician's eagerness to accomplish psychic feats of prowess, we sometimes observe a kind of addiction to psychic techniques. As one technique becomes pedestrian, so the student hungers for a new one to replace it, and so on up the illusory ladder of acquired techniques. This hunger becomes an outer distraction from the serious search for enlightenment, and it leads nowhere.

The teacher and mystic, Yoganada, cautioned his students when speaking of siddhis or yogic powers. "They are part of the spiritual path, but can become a major instrument of maya (illusion), resulting in the downfall of yogis who desire them. The spiritual path is not a circus."[3]

The magician must eventually come to understand that any physical manifestation, no matter how impressive, is but a symptom of the hidden mysteries of creation which are there to be discovered by those driven to learn its language. These particular sensitives are the ones who press on to an experience of the world of transcommunication.

Consciousness of the Medium

The true medium is the healer, the seer and the diviner.

In our tradition there are actually very few *true* mediums. In fact, you were never a medium until your teacher told you that you were a medium, for it is not a short road to understanding the hidden dynamics of time. It is not a short road to knowing the reality of worlds within worlds. But at the mediumistic consciousness, we know these things without a doubt and such knowledge enables us to divine without the intervention of the rational mind.

The consciousness of the medium moves beyond that of the magician, beyond that earnest apprentice whose manifestations are primarily psychic and who has a somewhat limited awareness of the spiritual implications of what they do.

The mind of the medium undergoes a transformation and becomes capable of transforming the world through inspiration. Humanity, as a whole, has benefitted from the mediumistic inspiration of many individuals throughout human history, in all cultures and all walks of life. We naturally think first of the artist, but we must also think of scientists like Baird, inventor of the mechanical television; Winchell, creator of the artificial heart; and Judson, who invented the ever-practical zipper. These were among the untold millions of everyday mediums who have been open to mediumistic inspiration.

A medium is not a communicator. A medium is a listener. A medium listens with complete attentiveness, without judgment, and then interprets these impressions for the recipient.

The medium's reality goes beyond that which can be seen from a worldly vantage point. There will ideally be an insight into the human experience from the perspective of body, soul and spirit. There will be an understanding of divine cause and effect, of the nature of eternity, and an awareness of the many worlds within worlds of creation itself which, although invisible to most, are more real to them than the illusion we call matter. There will be a growing experience of the soul, the spirit and the One. The named One. The One with many names.

The medium as the healer awakens the sense and soul of an individual to their own Beauty, so that they may then awaken to the beauty without. The work of healing mediums gave rise to the understanding of the human psyche, which then led on to the foundation of modern psychology.

Mediums are keepers of the mysteries of death. They understand that everything we do is acknowledged and that everyone we meet, both seen and unseen, we will meet again. Mediums know that every act is known.

Mediums are trained to embody and reawaken communion at every level – between people, between human beings in this world and the next, between our soul within and nature without, and ultimately between the spirit of all things.

Mediums are entrusted with the knowledge of the sacred power of the Word, made manifest in their ability to become inspired and to inspire others.

Those mediums who are on the pathway to the consciousness of the mystic know the reality of the etheric world. They are responsible for collaborating with the ancestors, for divining the future, for counselling the living, for inspiring and for manifesting healing in every act.

They are nomads of time and space. Our students often hear us use the word "etherea" rather than spirit world. It reflects our understanding that what we call the spirit world, commonly accepted as comprising souls who have passed on, is but one etheric reality among many. Those working within the mediumistic consciousness have come to understand that this physical world is but a world within worlds merging within Creation, and the medium moves between the worlds within a series of interconnecting realities. It is within these realms that the medium lives.

The medium is an intermediary between the etheric world and humankind, and awakens to the omnipresence of the Creator which echoes beyond and around every communication. In so doing, the medium embraces the sacred implications of the art of mediumship.

The awakening of the medium is lifelong.

Consciousness of the Mystic

It is the mystic who truly manifests magic – the magic that is God, the magic that is the Universe.

The path of the mystic is one of service. Dedication, discipline, meditation and contemplation move the mystic toward unity with the One, and within the One we may serve the many.

The passage from mediumistic to mystic consciousness moves the sensate individual to a place of psychic health, a passage which requires discipline, healing, knowledge, practice and a return to their nature. Within enlightenment, the Buddhist becomes a Buddha and the medium becomes a mystic. Only then does one have knowing of the many worlds of creation.

The medium as mystic is an instrument of transformation and revelation. Through gradual mystical unfoldment, the medium develops a profound receptiveness at the very deepest levels of his or her being. The medium as mystic begins to experience life spontaneously, breath by breath and movement by movement, becoming more pliable within and sensitive to the whispers of divine influence. Whereas the medium knows, the mystic understands. Such a pathway is not for the faint of heart, for mystical unfoldment comes about as a result of intense spiritual discipline and psychological challenges.

A mystic is awake to their frailties and their strengths, and knows how to achieve balance between them. Depth of wisdom develops as a result of a life lived fully in the world. By this we mean both esoterically and within their humanity as the mystic expresses their spirituality through their human talents and abilities.

The mystic seeks to bring balance to nature, whether that be within a person or within the world. The mystic also understands that we cannot look to the outcome, for everything is always at its beginning. The mystic seeks union with God. The mystic as mystagogue is capable of initiating others into the mysteries. The mystic is a keeper of sacred understanding and shares through revelation.

Should we choose to remain within the mechanics of the magician; to give message after message in answer to the emotional need of the human hearts that come to us; to stop our ears and hearts to the call of the soul's longing for this forward movement; then we deprive ourselves of an opportunity to leave the world of spiritual adolescence and enter spiritual adulthood.

For many such sensitives, eventual disillusionment with their craft is not uncommon, unconnected as they may have become to the vital spiritual source of their ability. But more importantly, consider those people who come to us seeking that communication with a loved one without truly understanding the experience they seek, and those desiring to understand the *meaning* behind the tragedies of their lives. Are they not grossly under-served by mechanical practice? The intention of a true medium should be to become the vehicle whereby one soul may touch another. The true medium goes beyond giving evidence to make the spirit presence felt, and thus allows healing to take place as it is needed between the souls of the individuals on both sides of the veil.

The whole point of phenomena is to wake us up, to awaken us to the presence of the One, to the mystical nature of life, and to stimulate our own divine nature into action for the benefit of our soul's expression.

The ability to move a table around the room is all well and good, but to move a soul toward its fulfilment is the work of God. It is important for those within the mediumistic consciousness to understand that, in this, we are more than magicians. Hopefully we may come to realise that we are God-centred and with that, are responsible for the spiritual implications of our ability.

> *"Phenomena are but the lenses through which*
> *we perceive God in ourselves."*
>
> Simon James

Persephone and Demeter

Demeter, goddess of the harvest, had a beautiful daughter called Persephone. Hades, Lord of the Underworld, wanting her for his own, caused the earth to open up and so abducted her. Broken hearted, Demeter wandered the earth looking for her daughter. In her great sorrow she caused the earth to become barren. Zeus, moved by the suffering of the starving people, sent Hermes down to Hades to bring Persephone home. But before giving her up, Hades tricked Persephone into eating pomegranate seeds which bound her to the Underworld forever. Henceforth she was forced to spend one third of each year there and, during this time of mourning, Demeter refused to let anything grow on earth. Thus, winter began.

Nature

Chapter Three:
Whence We Came

"I heard a voice, and the voice said..."

Simon James

Our Lineage

Most of the great religions of the world originated with someone who received an inspired communication from the Divine Intelligence, someone we now call a medium. The words received were intended to guide the human race toward fulfilling its spiritual potential. Such communications were meant to be a gateway to knowledge of the presence of the Divine on earth, encouraging our human journey into wholeness and our soul's journey toward God.

Looking back upon our vast lineage, it becomes clear that we may have lost sight of the original purpose of mediumship. True mediumship is the demonstration of living consciousness. Sadly, what we often see today is that mediumship has become a message-driven exhibition, or worse, an attractive career option. What was once a divine mystical event has now become largely a mechanical one.

It is our hope that, with knowledge and awareness, the essence of spirituality may once more infuse the noble practice of mediumship with the dignity that is its rightful heritage.

We come from an ancient theurgical tradition that embraces communion with the Divine as a pathway to God. Our work is an outflowing of esoteric knowledge deeply rooted in ancient spiritual thought and expressed throughout history's many cultural and religious traditions.

It may be helpful to say here that, when we speak of the esoteric nature of our work, we refer to its quality of obscurity and of its roots in mysticism. It is not intended to imply selectivity.

Although it is not our objective here to delve deeply into the many ancient philosophies themselves, perhaps an overview of what our mediumistic heritage actually looks like may shed some light on the intrinsically devotional nature of the intuitive arts.

Ancient Disciplines

We are part of a modern theurgical tradition. We embody and seek the *thread of truth* that runs through all the great ancient schools of thought.

We can trace the fundamental elements of our modern esoteric heritage back through movements such as Alchemy, Christianity, Gnosticism and Hermeticism, and within the Kabbalist, Bon, Greek, Celtic and Spiritualist traditions. Certain fundamental truths run through all of these schools of thought. They are connected by some common threads which are expressed differently within each culture.

That said, we attempt to go beyond these cultural beliefs and connect with the essence of those profound truths which have sustained human spiritual integrity throughout the generations.

Prophecy and direct spirit counsel are recurring phenomena in most religious philosophies and are generally responsible for their very creation. Judaism speaks of the divine inspiration received by the prophet Moses and, in Hinduism, that received by Arjuna. The common thread of truth we seek lies in understanding that, within the voice of God or the gods, is to be found that which animates the spiritual life of all humanity since the beginning of time.

Traditionally, mediums are trained to recognise these diverse outer cultural expressions. Our job is to see beyond cultural differences and to follow that inherent thread of the Spirit. Only then can we properly serve someone within their particular understanding.

We, as teaching mediums, are regularly consulted by other religious and metaphysical leaders from around the world who recognise that the sacred knowledge we have inherited, and for which we are guardians, goes beyond religion, creed or cultural belief.

In seeking the underlying thread of truth, we must also have an acute awareness of what our own cultural perceptions are. It is a lifelong discipline that takes thought, practice and courage. To this end, we believe that the training of a true medium is not just about acquiring a skill set, but is rather a transformative experience in which the medium comes to know his or her true nature, beyond cultural perception. In doing so, we may then come to see through the mask of another human being to their spiritual essence, whether they be of this world or the next, and consequently we may truly serve the needs of their spirit.

Modern Mystery Schools

In more recent times, the continuity of our esoteric lineage may be found in the work of philosophers such as Emanuel Swedenborg in Europe and Andrew Jackson Davis in America. They were but two of the many truth seekers who strove to share their awareness of spiritual reality, in contradiction to prevailing religious doctrines of the 18th and 19th centuries.

By the early 1800's, the Quakers, Universalists, Shakers and other New Thought movements were thriving in the United States, manifesting and recording mediumistic phenomena and thereby sowing the seeds for a tide of spiritual change. One such event in 1848 might be considered the moment when spirit communication went viral. The Hydesville rappings, as they became known, were the spark which ignited the flame of a worldwide movement called Modern Spiritualism. It was the tipping point of collective consciousness when once again, as in ancient times, the etheric world made yet another attempt to reach the collective human heart through the mind of a medium. The subsequent deterioration of what should have been a great spiritual movement into an arena for public spectacle is one of the sad realities of the age. It is our hope to reclaim the divine dignity which is the birthright of what began as a great spiritual awakening.

Similarly, modern advocates of the New Age movement may be interested to learn that they can trace their beginnings to another 19th century movement called Theosophy, established by an occultist by the name of Madame Helena Blavatsky. Thus, the threads of connection interweave. It seems that the New Age movement is not so very new at all.

Transcommunication has a supreme healing purpose – that is, to provide verification that no one is forsaken. No one is forgotten. No one is overlooked. In the eyes of God, all are seen and therefore all are equal. The vigorous social activism which characterised the religious movements of this era arose out of this belief, for we cannot morally have it one way in etherea and another in the physical world.

The act of sharing these spiritual ethics through the demonstration of mediumship is a great privilege accompanied by a responsibility to exemplify these principles in our lives as well as in our word. The original tenets of this lineage, when properly understood, are the medium's natural creed and philosophy. However, it does not mean that any one spiritual philosophy holds exclusive entitlement to all mystical knowledge. Quite the contrary. That said, the practice of mediumship holds a valued place within these traditions as an expression of human equality and of the continuity of the soul beyond death.

Historically, divination, intuition and mediumship were largely processes of initiation into the mysteries of creation. Such was the tremendous power of the ancient mediums that they were able to heal, to raise the mists and to affect the natural elements. However, these phenomena were but outward manifestations of the profound inner spiritual knowledge they sought. A demonstration of mediumship, as it is typically carried out today, will neither evoke an awakening to the mysteries nor create a divine moment. The true mystical experience is to be found, not in a message-driven demonstration, but rather within the environment created through spiritual discipleship and a depth of wisdom.

Today, our understanding of the essence of mediumship and the very reason for its existence is somewhat wanting. But more than ever, it is needed. Mediumship, when used merely to demonstrate evidence of an afterlife, and goes no further, is a dead end. Mediumship is rooted in the psychic faculty and, if it remains only that, we shall continue to perform the tricks rather than manifesting the Presence – the Presence that truly moves and heals. The execution of mechanics does not make the medium. It only exercises the talent.

We can all agree that verification is paramount in the practice of mediumship; but it is the richnesses that lie beneath the evidence, the revelation of immortal existence that brings the act of mediumship to life and gives the gift of healing to all who bear witness.

What does the demonstration of mediumship reveal to us about the nature of the Great Spirit? What does the fact of survival tell us about the natural blueprint of the universe? These are the revelations for which true mediumship exists.

We encourage you to move from being the mechanic to the magician, from the magician to the medium – one who embraces transformation of self within the mystical understanding.

Ours is an oral tradition, handed down from teacher to student. We reiterate that, in our tradition, you were not a medium until your teacher called you a medium. This is because until you understood your spiritual roots, of which mediumship was only an outward expression, you were not a true medium.

In recent times, however, a wave of spiritual shopping seems to have come upon us. There appears to be a reluctance to commit to a discipline and an unsettling tendency to be swayed by concepts that make us feel good but require little actual work. Many of the so-called higher teachings derive from half-heard Spiritualist principles of long ago, regurgitated for modern consumption like spiritual baby food with little need to chew.

We would ask that a worker for the Spirit go deeper. Those within the mediumistic consciousness understand what lies behind the expression, are willing to do the personal work needed, and are moved to understand the rich spiritual implications of the art they are so privileged to practise.

How Odin Lost His Eye

The god Odin, troubled by prophecies of the end of the cosmos, went in search of Mimir. Mimir was the keeper of the mead of wisdom, held within the well which lay deep within the roots of the great tree, Yggdrasil. Mimir never asked anything less than the right eye of anyone who would drink of the mead. Odin drank, and in so doing gained the wisdom he sought. He then plucked out his eye and Mimir tossed it into the well, where it shone from its depths as a sign to all of the price to be paid for true insight.

Sacrifice

Chapter Four:
Alchemy of the Soul

"To the spiritually awakened consciousness of man,
every blade of grass is a message of love from the great Over Soul."

Julia Schlesinger[1]

Spiritual Transformation

According to Hermetic philosophy, which is the wellspring of our lineage, alchemy comprises one of the three parts of the wisdom of the universe. The word alchemy comes from the Greek meaning "the art of transmuting metals." This ancient practice was concerned with converting base metals into gold and with the magical implications of wielding power to create and transform matter.

In our tradition, the alchemical principles are woven deeply within our approach to the development and practice of esoteric transcommunication. For us, this has everything to do with the spiritual transformation of the soul. We do not separate our inner spiritual growth from our outer practice, either in daily life or in mediumship.

The Hermetic philosophy of "as above, so below" says that we are a reflection of God, and God is a reflection of us. That being so, our outer practice can only have the healing emanation we seek when our inner being is whole. We are ever striving to stand in our Beauty.

All creation flows from the Great Architect. Creation is a conscious, ever-evolving, interrelated whole. Each creative spark of the Divine comes to know itself through an orderly unfoldment toward our divine nature. To each and every soul is given the privilege of eternal progression, and as we manifest our spirit through soul and the physical body, so we then make our way back again to the Source in an infinite cycle.

"As above, so below." To this, we ourselves add, "as within, so without." For the evolution of the universe is mirrored in the evolution of life on earth, just as the life we have created for ourselves is a reflection of our inner reality. There is a divine unified pattern here, a divine intelligence. We shall begin to become aware that what we traditionally understand as the etheric world is but one world within many worlds, connected by the creative movement of the Great Spirit. As the 19th century seer, Andrew Jackson Davis said, "The outer universe is a visible manifestation of the Indwelling Deity. Nature is the body, God is the soul."[2]

The mediumistic path to the mystic is, in essence, the pursuit of enlightenment or gnosis. In *Hymns of Hermes*, G.R.S. Mead defines gnosis as, "the experience of liberating interior knowledge."[3] It suggests that we consciously disengage from all that is not in unity with the One. In doing so, what remains is an awakened state which is, in fact, the divine reality.

The ancestral roots of our particular theurgic tradition can be traced back to Pythagoras, Aristotle, Plato and the Hermetic philosophers, among others. As exponents of this lineage, our teaching and practice is a natural blend of philosophical and religious thought in which the medium's inner unfoldment and the medium's outer practice are ideally one and the same. As within, so without.

Therefore, we believe that the study of the levels of consciousness and the personifications which predated the notion of archetypes, is fundamental to the development of the true medium. In fact, until the 1920s it was taught as a core component of intuitive practice. Development took place over a period of many years, in somewhat disquieting contrast to the modern trend of short seminars. In recent years, the absence of these teachings within our field has resulted in a tendency on the part of the spiritual seeker to search for evidence of our own mysteries in those of other cultures, religions and philosophies.

And so, it becomes our hope to bring back the magic, to rediscover the mysteries within our own theurgic lineage and to integrate them back into our everyday lives as mediums and sensate practitioners in all walks of life.

Above all, the understanding of archetypes is a tool of transformation. Its primary function, in our way, has everything to do with the power that this knowledge brings to move us into the balance of our own nature as human beings, as healers and as mediums. The truth and wisdom engendered within us affect the quality of our own lives as we move toward enlightenment. And as we emanate this quality of healing within our being, it affects the healing we may bring to others, whatever our mode of practice. This is soul work in its essence.

Secondarily, an understanding of archetypes within the mediumistic tradition is paramount especially as it relates to guides, trance work and archetypal projection because it hones the intuitive's ability to discern between wishful thinking and reality. The critical faculty combined with an open heart makes for a promising basis from which we may ascertain the truth.

Levels of Consciousness

Before looking at some of the pivotal archetypes within traditional mediumship, we turn to the four basic aspects of the human condition, or levels of consciousness, and learn to observe their manifestation in ourselves and in others.

Symbolically, a mystic orders the evolution of consciousness into progressive steps much like those of a pyramid, with mineral consciousness at its base, and moving upwards through vegetable and animal consciousness toward human consciousness at the peak.

Obviously, this is an inadequate representation of what is a divine model, and we do not suggest in any way that humans have dominion over creation. For in our tradition, every blade of grass is sentient and no state of being can be compared to another. There is no common hierarchy of soul progression by which all souls are measured. We speak only of the quality or nature of consciousness at each stage through which we all pass. Within each lifetime is the opportunity for enlightenment according to the individual's divine impulse. Certainly, the medium's job is to be awake to this awareness, but never to judge. That said, our symbolic model may help us to more fully understand the unfoldment of human consciousness.

In esoteric understanding, all things have consciousness. Consciousness works through the biology of our being. Consciousness is both separate from and interdependent upon our physical existence.

Consciousness implies innate awareness and communication. All things express consciousness through their energy. Living cells, rocks, vegetation, all have a distinct energetic makeup and therefore emanate differently. The elements of earth, air, fire and water have their unique properties of consciousness. They are "aware." Nothing is exempt.

Here then, outlined in the broadest of brushstrokes, are the four fundamental levels of consciousness to which we refer:

> *Mineral State or Survival:* The instinct for food, shelter and sex. The physical vessel is concerned with its own survival and the continuity of the species. Most of the world's population functions within this state of being.

Vegetable State or Gathering: The need for growth and security after chaos, and for staying put geographically to accomplish this. Many of our ancestors did precisely this after the world wars and the Great Depression, amassing goods and securing a material future for their children.

Animal State or Power: Once secure and comfortable, we then seek power both within ourselves and in the outer world. There is more geographical movement here, a desire for material gain for the purposes of status rather than survival, as well as inner movement toward consciousness of self.

Human State or Knowledge: When acquisitions no longer satisfy us, we search for knowledge. We turn from the outer world to the inner reality, to spirituality, in a quest to understand our divine nature. In our tradition, we seek what we call the *Point of the Heart* or the realm of the God Nature.

Movement from one state of awareness to another can be observed during the lifetime of a single individual, over a period of time within a culture, or as a direct outcome of economic strife within a nation.

As a working intuitive, it is of considerable value to be aware of the balance of these conditions within the individual with whom you are working, and as it relates to the culture from which they come. Keep in mind that one condition is not superior to another and that aspects of each condition exist in varying degrees within every human being.

Archetypes

In the mystic's way, knowledge has been handed down orally from teacher to student, for good reason. Mystical knowledge cannot truly be known and understood except through experience, and that experience must be safely nurtured in the presence of teachers who have themselves unfolded in the esoteric ways. This is particularly true when we begin to touch upon archetypes in mystical mediumship.

A great many books have been written on the subject of archetypes, though none yet sufficiently explore its function as it pertains to mediumship. In more recent times, the work of psychologist Carl Jung brought the idea of archetypes into public awareness as a way of investigating the psyche and thereby fostering the healthy mental development of the individual. Those who have researched Jung's early career will attest to his thorough study of certain aspects of mysticism and mediumship, as a prelude to developing his psychotherapeutic methods.

Although the root of Jung's work in archetypes is to be found within our mediumistic heritage, the similarity ends there. The first of Brian Robertson's esteemed life mentors, Ray H. Woollam, stated, "The only point to self-examination is that the self, upon examination, immediately disappears. Any other so-called self-examination is not a 'turning-to-look-in' at all. Rather, it is merely the retelling of that ancient and continuing illusion of self-image."

For us, the archetypes in our tradition serve as a pathway to God, taking the human being beyond the psyche, on a journey from soul to spirit. That said, we share a common intention. Jung's ultimate purpose, and ours, is to heal.

In our tradition an archetype is an inherent pattern of being. The pattern creates a symbolic "personage" with predominant characteristics that hold certain associations and meanings for us. These patterns are often universally agreed upon and can be reflective of an individual, a tribe, a culture or humanity as a whole. Put another way, an archetype is a created persona that embodies a set of specific universal characteristics.

In this volume we shall touch only briefly upon this vast area of exploration. Mediums who work with trance mediumship, however, are well advised to be aware of the existence of these realms in order that they may discern the active presence of archetypal manifestation both within themselves and as they observe archetypal embodiment in others whom they serve.

There are nine archetypes in our tradition, eight of which emanate from the central ninth, which is your Beauty. Each archetype has its associated quality, planet, direction, element, age range, season and weather. Each archetype also has an associated movement that is passed down from teacher to student when the student is ready. The movements themselves, when taught in conjunction with certain intentions, activate the energetic qualities of the archetype and heighten the experience within.

With the clear understanding that what follows is but the tip of the iceberg, we share here our original, simplified, visual representation of the traditional archetypes. For our present purposes, we will touch upon four of the nine archetypes.

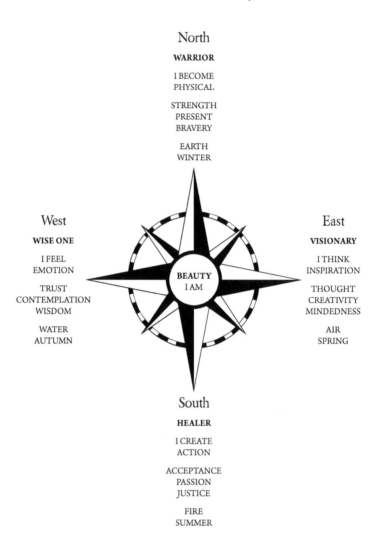

North

WARRIOR

I BECOME
PHYSICAL

STRENGTH
PRESENT
BRAVERY

EARTH
WINTER

West

WISE ONE

I FEEL
EMOTION

TRUST
CONTEMPLATION
WISDOM

WATER
AUTUMN

BEAUTY
I AM

East

VISIONARY

I THINK
INSPIRATION

THOUGHT
CREATIVITY
MINDEDNESS

AIR
SPRING

South

HEALER

I CREATE
ACTION

ACCEPTANCE
PASSION
JUSTICE

FIRE
SUMMER

Within each of us can be found aspects of these archetypes in greater or lesser prominence. At the neutral centre, we find you in your Beauty, in that perfect point of balance and stillness wherein the soul is at peace. Here, you sit as the observer, the watcher. You sit at the junction of the seen and unseen worlds in a position from which you act rather than react. You are in your true nature, the "I Am".

Remember always, that the mystic's path is just that, a path, not a result. We have all of eternity to travel its glorious length. The mystic is ever moving toward Beauty, or true self, through healing. We are ever becoming.

> In the east, we find the Visionary with its qualities of creativity, imagination and communication. This is the mind of the Inspirer, the "I Think", where we express our true talents. As an aspect of spring, it is associated with childhood which, in our way, encompasses ages 1 to 27 years.
>
> In the south is the Healer. This is where we step into acceptance where all healing begins. Here we discover passion and action, as "I Create". The Healer is centred in the heart. As an aspect of summer, it is associated with young adulthood, ages 27 to 54 years.
>
> In the west is the Wise One, the "I Feel", embodying knowledge, experience, wisdom, compassion and understanding. The Wise One waits, listens and receives. The Wise One emerges only to the extent that healing has taken place. As an aspect of autumn, it is associated with adulthood, ages 54 to 81 years.
>
> In the north, we step into the Warrior, the "I Become", the hero and the defender. The Warrior embodies true strength which comes about only as a result of the wisdom gained through experience. The Warrior walks in truth and manifests courage, authority and patience. An aspect of winter, it is associated with elderhood, ages 81 years and onwards.

For the medium, the benefits of exploring the archetypes are profound and lie partly in their tremendous potential to create balance within us. The work begins once we recognise the dominance of the archetypal qualities within ourselves and then allow one to balance the other in order to heal. To use a mundane example, if we are lacking in confidence, we may activate the qualities of the Warrior; if a recipient is in great emotional distress, we as mediums may step into the Healer in order to effect a peace of mind – if we are trained to do so. These are but muted illustrations of what is a boundless, dynamic heritage of esoteric knowledge.

Once again, we are ever striving and never arriving. There are, nevertheless, endless joyous platforms along the way where we celebrate the creativity and self-fullness that comes about as we work toward the unfolding of our nature and our Beauty.

One of the reasons we value true trance mediumship is that we prize the wisdom that it makes available to us, bringing forth words of inspiration and healing that seem to elude us in our normal state of waking consciousness. However, if the medium is unfamiliar with their archetypal patterns, which are more often than not the actual source of communication in the altered state, it might be natural to assume that these great thoughts have been spoken by a spirit guide or an entity quite separate from themselves.

With all due respect to those intuitive practitioners confident in their ability to identify a person's spirit guide we can reasonably state that, in a great many cases, these identified guides are simply archetypal projections of the person which have been picked up by the practitioner. Neither is it uncommon for novice workshop participants, for example, to invoke the archetype within themselves and call it a guide. Unfortunately, as long as one always believes it to be an entity separate from oneself, one's own soul potential cannot be fully realised. We do not say spirit guides do not exist, for they most certainly do. We suggest, however, that they simply do not pop up with the frequency that the more fanciful of practitioners might claim.

It is a matter of being honest about our observations and keen in our powers of discernment. Keeping a rational and fair mind will not only enhance your own development as a medium, but afford the recipient of your work an opportunity for real healing.

Besides, is it not worth your consideration that there is more to your own spirit than you may have understood? Contemplate the possibility that your soul is possessed of a wealth of insight you may not normally access. Knowledge and experience of the archetypal patterns inherent within you provide the potential for profound guidance, provided the subject is ethically taught by those with knowledge.

Why would we prefer to consult a separate guide or entity when there is a most remarkable kingdom within us? We suggest that the human spirit and the human soul are possessed of infinite potential for spiritual vision.

As Andrew Jackson Davis observed, speaking not about our guides but about ourselves as human beings, "Self is the portal through which the soul looks into the far off."[4]

The Book of Thoth

Neferkaptah, son of the King of Egypt, was a magician who cared for little else but to acquire knowledge. He coveted the lost Book of Thoth which contained all the world's magic. He who possessed it gained mastery of all the elements and could understand the language of all the earth's creatures.

One day, having paid much gold to discover the Book's whereabouts, Neferkaptah set sail with his wife and son and, finding the place where it lay at the bottom of the Nile, used his magic to raise it to the surface. As he opened the Book, he at once enchanted all the elements and understood the language of all creatures.

But Thoth, enraged at the loss of his Book, caused Neferkaptah, his wife and his son to be drawn overboard on their homeward journey, and they were all drowned. Thus, in his eagerness, Neferkaptah forfeited his life, his loved ones and, indeed, the very mysteries he sought.

Reverence

Chapter Five:
Spirituality and Mediumship

"When you reach that spiritual consciousness
of the powers belonging to your own spirit,
then you open the door into the spiritual state."

J.J. Morse[1]

Illumination of the Soul

Spirituality. The word itself implies many things to many people. For the purposes of this book, we will speak of it as it relates to our work as mediums and sensitives.

It does not necessarily follow that a practising medium or psychic is a spiritually aware individual. The intuitive faculty, technically speaking, can be exercised without any awareness of its inherent interweaving with Spirit and spirituality. However, this disconnection can be precarious.

Those who seek clarity from an intuitive generally arrive in a state of extreme vulnerability and usually assume that the practitioner is automatically spiritually grounded and equipped with a degree of spiritual insight. Such a common assumption may be forgiven as we see some practitioners package themselves in the guise of spirituality, draped in shades of purple and sporting an impressive array of gemstones.

The fact remains, however, that unless the practitioner has an understanding of the divine nature of the art we practise and its spiritual implications, great harm can be done to the psyche of persons both here and in the afterlife. The consequences of thoughtless statements prompted by ego or a need to feel powerful can be devastating to the soul of the recipient. At the very least, we as mediums are morally bound to cause no suffering.

Mediumship was intended to further the spiritual empowerment of the human race. It is fervently to be hoped that mediumship and psychic faculties may be employed in the way in which they were intended; that is, to bring healing to the world.

Mediumship is not a gift. It is a faculty. It exists, in part, to serve as the vehicle for communication with those in the etheric world. They are always our first priority. We must be mindful that this may be the only opportunity they ever have to speak to their loved ones on the earth. In listening carefully to their needs, we may be privileged to provide comfort and to aid in their healing. Working with compassionate intent also opens up pathways to the unfoldment of the medium's own spirit, furthering his or her own relationship with the Divine.

Mediumship is about listening. It should be every medium's priority to listen to the true intent of the communicator, without overlaying, adding to, or avoiding the meaning that is intended. It is his or her duty to relay with honesty and integrity that which has been received. What may to the medium be a seemingly inconsequential piece of evidence may be, for the spirit communicator and the recipient, the very piece of the puzzle that sets healing in motion.

Our task is to provide verification of the magnificent truth that the etheric world is but an extension of this existence in a different form. Once we know and understand that life continues beyond the moment we call death, this earthly life becomes all the more precious. Eternity does not begin when we die. We are creating our eternity now, because we are spirit now. We have the tremendous gift of freedom to create our own reality, both here and hereafter.

Why develop the mediumistic faculty? Ask yourself, "What is my intention? What is my motive for wanting to develop my sensitivity?" Assuming that the natural ability is already there, you may wish to examine the reasons for wanting to develop it. The first response is generally, "I want to help people," which is undoubtedly a fine motive and not one to be taken lightly. Closer examination, however, may sometimes uncover other less conscious motives.

As we dig deeper, it is not uncommon to find that the natural ego may play an equally significant part in our wish to become mediums. The basic human desire to be recognised is undoubtedly satisfied a hundredfold at the thought of being a voice for the spirit world. The potential public allure is unmistakable. After all, who would not wish to be regarded as a "gifted" individual, a special agent of the Divine revered by the many?

If we can but remember that we are all seen and heard by the Divine Being, and that no one goes unacknowledged by the Great Spirit; if we can but remember that our intimate and direct connection with the God of Our Own Understanding makes us special beyond any degree of esteem that could possibly be conferred by the public; then we may realise that fame and fortune are of no real consequence whatsoever. As with any other human endeavour, our motivation needs to be spiritually healthy or our ability will eventually suffer.

It must be said that transcommunication is not now, and never was, intended to promote celebrity. Unfortunately, techniques that often pass for mediumship have caused more harm to the human psyche than is presently understood. Poor mediumship and fraud have wreaked havoc upon the profound spiritual truths expressed within many traditional religious philosophies. Their inherent integrity has been tainted by the worship of the spirit world rather than God.

In our present day and age, the cult of media celebrity has done little to remedy this state of affairs, focusing as it does upon sensationalism and fear mongering. In addition, when the medium's personal need for public acclaim is first on their agenda and service to humanity takes a back seat, they have abused their divine heritage. Mediums are born and unfolded to be of service to the etheric world.

It may interest you to know that the great 19th century orator, Emma Hardinge Britten was inspired by the spirit to curtail her public demonstrations in favour of private sittings and teaching; so doing reinforced the act of mediumship as a vehicle of healing rather than a spectacle. Even Andrew Jackson Davis found the growing obsession with phenomena to be a distraction to the true purpose of mediumship. Both Hardinge Britten and Davis understood that, while the magician may glorify the spirit world, the mystic honours the Divine. The medium exists to do the work of the Creator by connecting with the etheric world. In fact, the word "religion", currently a most unpopular concept, simply means "to bind back"; in other words, to reconnect the individual with God. And should this not be our prime aspiration as mediums?

Thus, even in the 19th century, the spirit world was prophesying that message-driven public demonstrations would lead to the degradation of the sacred act of spirit communication. Unfortunately, that which was forecast has come to be. In every aspect of our daily work as teachers and practising mediums, as lecturers and healers, our ultimate goal is to revive the reverence, to revive the sacred purpose that yet lies dormant within the art of transcommunication.

So then, why become a medium? Why spend the years of discipline, sacrifice and emotional toil that it takes to become a true medium?

The motive can only be to serve the One, etherea and humanity. The unasked-for gift will be that of your own enlightenment and your own burgeoning relationship with the God of Your Own Understanding.

Can we practise mediumship without attention to our spirituality? The answer is yes, of course; but the reality is that we may inadvertently cause suffering to others in the absence of spiritual awareness. It also puts our own ability in jeopardy over the long run.

It must be stated once again that, just because someone has a mediumistic ability, it does not automatically follow that they are spiritually aware. A glance at the majority of today's celebrity psychics is a glaring case in point. In fact, spirituality and the psychic faculty are not necessarily connected at all.

From time to time as mediums, we ourselves have been invited to work with indigenous people from different cultures around the world, sharing our respective mystical traditions. On one occasion, we were asked to dance with them before we started working together. They wanted to see if we were authentic teachers! Because if they couldn't see certain rhythmic aspects within our movement and if a person wasn't in their own rhythm, in their own Beauty, then they knew we were not truly with the Creator. They wouldn't actually take on our teaching until they saw that. Likewise, some of you have often heard us say, only partly in jest, "Never trust a teacher who can't dance!"

All energy is rhythm, and those within the mediumistic consciousness need to recognise rhythm: the rhythm of one's own energy and the energy of life. A medium must truly understand that. When we urge you to "dance in the joy of the Spirit" we understand that we are connecting with that energy. It not only enhances unity with God, but enhances the harmony of our own nature.

Transcommunication is a faculty, a part of your soul's expression. Having this talent does not make you any more special than a good parent, a good cook, a good pianist, or a good plumber. It simply makes you more sensitive to the choices that you do make and amplifies their impact upon you and those around you. With this in mind then, surely the impetus arises to strengthen your spiritual understanding in order that your ability may become resilient, balanced and enduring.

The spiritually aware medium has a responsibility. The very act of connecting a discarnate soul with an incarnate one has profound ethical and spiritual ramifications. A responsible medium will be aware that he or she is touching an energy that profoundly shapes and affects the spirits of all three parties, and that great healing or harm can result depending on the medium's spiritual awareness.

In the early days of the telephone, a switchboard operator manually plugged in a line from the caller to the corresponding socket belonging to the recipient, making an electrical connection between the two. The operator then informed the recipient of the caller's identity. Assuming that the recipient did not hang up, the ensuing conversation would hopefully be meaningful for both parties. So far, the switchboard operator has opened the lines of communication. But the real substance of the communication begins when one voice is recognised by the other.

So it is with mediumship. The data or evidence given, however impressive, is much like the plug in the socket. This connection, when done well, captures the attention of the recipient and quickens the resolve of the communicator. But the real healing only takes place when the actual conversation begins and the soul of each party is stirred.

Mechanical mediumship consists of putting the plug in the socket and identifying the caller. Many may dazzle us with the sheer quantity, speed and accuracy of the act of connection. This is, without a doubt, a skill of tremendous value. Mediumship in its truest sense, however, not only provides verification; it then seeks to understand the soul's need underneath the evidence. The developing mediumistic consciousness listens for those deeper currents of meaning hidden behind the mask of the communicator which, when sensitively communicated, can create the healing that is sought by the caller.

Again, here we see the difference between the consciousness of the magician and that of the medium.

The only way we can truly understand spirituality is through our own experience. Therefore, if a medium chooses to avoid the honest development of his or her own spiritual nature and instead opts to manipulate the mechanics of psychism and mediumship for personal motives, he or she has sadly missed out on the great privilege of being in service to etherea and to the Divine. On the other hand, when we make the conscious choice to awaken our spiritual nature, we awaken the whole world.

The very existence of psychism and mediumship implies a power beyond our rational comprehension, and in the act of mediumship we cannot help but sense the presence of the Spirit. Surely this is our first clue that the development of our personal spirituality is paramount if we are to become clear channels for the expression of the God Presence.

What we do is a spiritual action. It has ethical, spiritual and metaphysical implications. We have a responsibility primarily to those in the afterlife who trust us to communicate their thoughts truthfully, without embellishment or reserve. We have a secondary responsibility to the incarnate soul in front of us. As long as what we do is about service, and as long as we do the best we can with the awareness we have, the foundations for ethical practice are laid. It is a good beginning.

It then becomes our utmost responsibility to develop our inner spirituality in tandem with our talents. The balanced expansion of these two qualities will move us toward the greatest possible fulfillment of our potential, and make us more worthy instruments of service to the spirits, incarnate and discarnate.

Remember, you are touching worlds upon worlds. You are piercing the energy of another person and, make no mistake, it will leave its mark. You are indeed playing with fire. The ramifications to your own spirit and to those in both worlds are profound.

We repeat that, although the theurgic tradition we practise is not the only pathway of spiritual development, it is particularly suited to the journey of the sensate individual, embodying those essential threads of truth that run through many of the world's great schools of divine thought, minus the dogma. Rather than repress areas of discord within us, we are asked to look squarely at our own frailties and strengths and to take responsibility for our personal growth as spiritual human beings. So doing encourages that inner awareness that is so essential to the development of a healthy medium.

We know that this earthly life is a precious but temporary state of being which makes up part of our eternal progression as we move toward becoming a fuller and truer expression of the God Nature. The spirit of all creatures is eternal and cannot die. The soul, on the other hand, is the temporary expression of the spirit within us. Metaphorically speaking, the soul sits between the choices of the mind and the call of the spirit.

Within our free will we may choose either change or inertia, growth or complacency, healing or suffering. The decisions we make today set in motion the causes of the effects we live tomorrow. These choices determine the extent to which we unfold at any given time along our eternal path. Some of us may follow the inner impulse for change while others resist or ignore it altogether. In either instance, our spirit will ultimately achieve its destiny in eternity, just as iron filings are inevitably drawn toward a magnet. How painful or pleasurable that journey is depends upon our degree of willingness to surrender to the Divine Will.

Those of us who seek a spiritual life, who wish to touch the divine heartbeat of creation, must allow movement. Movement is change. Sometimes we only move when things are no longer comfortable for us. Those of us who seek a spiritual life do so because we are no longer content with what was. We must move. In doing so, we choose to embrace the changes that bring us back to our true nature. The conscious intention to unfold our true nature and thereby reveal more of the divine within us is a choice of the mind, prompted by the movement of the soul, to fulfil the destiny of the spirit.

The path of a medium is the path of a lifelong novice, ever learning, ever at the beginning, ever the initiate. The development of the mediumistic faculty is exquisitely linked to the illumination of the soul. Personal healing and mediumistic development must therefore go hand in hand.

Whatever path you choose, choose the one that brings you to your honesty, that encourages no lies about your agenda, that brings out the best in your humanity, and that supports your compassionate intention.

True mediumship is God-centred, not self-centred. Choose the path of spiritual service.

Odin and the Wisdom of the Runes

The god Odin desired to know the secrets of the runes carved into the roots of the great tree, Yggdrasil. The runes contained the secrets of the cosmos and influenced every aspect of the Nine Worlds. This knowledge was revealed only to those who proved themselves worthy of such fearful insight.

So Odin hung himself from a branch of Yggdrasil, pierced himself with his spear, and for nine days and nights peered into the waters beneath the tree. At the end of the ninth night, the runes accepted his sacrifice and revealed their secrets to him. Thus was Odin initiated into the mysteries.

Discipline

Chapter Six:
Nature of the Intuitive Arts

"Wisdom is the sum of all knowledge, the application of all truth,
the willing performance of all duties; in short, the harmonious
adjustment of the finite Ego to the infinite I Am."

Elizabeth Lowe Watson[1]

Three Aspects of Being

We now turn to some aspects of esoteric theory which we trust may help to throw light upon the real meaning of some fundamental elements of our art. The so-called New Age concepts that have flooded our bookshelves in recent times, and those feel-good buzz words which have been bandied about so freely, are often confusing and sometimes misleading to the sincere seeker after truth. For a medium, clarity of thought is paramount. And so we shall touch upon some of the more essential ideas which go to make up the foundations of the work of an intuitive.

Within our present view, we acknowledge three primary aspects of our being: the spirit, the soul and the physical body.

Your spirit is the eternal spark of the Divine, that unchangeable aspect of yourself which is the God Nature, the "I Am."

The soul is the vehicle of the spirit expressing itself through the incarnation of your physical body, itself comprising three interpenetrating systems: matter, emotional energy and mental energy. Put another way, the soul is the "medium" of the spirit. It is imprinted with all that we ever were and everything that we have become: mind and emotions, experiences and memories, personality and identity. These layers of energy and vibration are constantly in motion, constantly changing and make up that dynamic condition we call Life.

This interweaving of soul and body constitutes what we sometimes call the subtle or etheric body. The etheric body emanates what is known as the aura.

Looking now at the complete picture, at this wondrous, interdependent dance of spirit, soul and body, is it not a perfect symphony? Surely we cannot be physical bodies who just happen to possess a soul. But rather, we are spiritual beings who have been blessed with a physical body through which to give the soul the right set of circumstances to express the spirit. Your spirit.

Power and Energy

You cannot be where the Presence of God is not.

Understood more correctly, what is often called the Power is, in our way, the Presence of God, or the God-power. It is the underlying communal force, the unified field that permeates all things, seen and unseen. It is eternal and constant and unaffected by time, space or circumstance. The God-power is ever present, and the Presence is infinite.

The more you surrender to the Presence, sit in the Presence and live in the Presence, the greater will be your awareness of it.

How do we differentiate between God-power and energy? The true answer is through experience. But for the sake of clarity, let's look at a simple example.

A tree comprises bark, roots, branches and leaves – all visible attributes of the invisible energy that thrusts the tree upward from its earthbound seedling, and which transforms the energy of the sun into the physical energy needed for the tree to grow. But it is the God-power which *animates* the energy. It is the infinite source from which is drawn all lesser manifestations of energy, both visible and invisible. It animates the tree and is shared by all trees. It is Nature. It is God.

Our awareness of the Presence may be amplified by prayer, by the practice of healing mediumship, through intention, or when we sit for the Presence of the Spirit.

Energy, on the other hand, is an aspect of force inherent within all beings and objects which can be transformed but never destroyed. To an intuitive, everything is energy. The nature, quality and degree of the energy emitted by a being or object is communicated by means of its *vibration*. In simple terms, this vibration creates what is referred to as the aura which, emanating from the soul energy of the individual, contains information that may be perceived by a sensitive.

Energy is in a constant state of flux. Its effects are finite. It varies in intensity depending upon factors such as time, circumstance and location. For example, if you have eaten very little on a particular day your physical energy may wane; if you have expended emotional energy you may feel drained. A building may be more energetically "charged" if the activities carried on within its walls over time have resulted in a reservoir of energy that lingers.

Energy belongs to the material realm even though it is invisible. With skill, it can be manipulated as in psychokinesis, or transformed as in healing. As always, it is a natural force that commands respectful use for ethical purposes.

To use another example, in a demonstration of mediumship the energy is ideally provided by the listeners who, it is to be hoped, emanate a sense of goodwill and respect. In this way, an ocean of energy is created in which the medium may swim, activating the awareness of the Presence. Remember that you cannot be where the Presence is not. However, we seek to provide the energetic circumstances to amplify our awareness of it for the purposes of communication between worlds. As always, it must be borne in mind that along with these abilities comes a great moral responsibility.

We can manipulate the nature of energy but we cannot manipulate the nature of the God-power although, with experience, we may learn to use energy to direct its flow, as in mediumistic healing.

> Energy is the material expression of the Power.
> The Power is the Presence of the Spirit.
> The Spirit is the presence of God.

Soul and Spirit

When we speak of esoteric things, we sometimes use words which can easily become meaningless through casual use. It is important to be clear about what we mean when speaking of soul and spirit, especially when we are working with the precious human soul here and in the etheric world.

The Great Spirit. The Infinite Intelligence, the God of Your Own Understanding, the Divine Power – whatever words we use, we are speaking of the source of all things. In our present day and age, the word God has evidently fallen out of favour due to negative associations and prejudices. But the fact remains that, whatever one chooses to call It – the Universal Mind, the Divine, the God Mind – we are referring to that which animates all things. We are naming the One.

Spirit. Again, we refer here to the Divine Presence. When written, a capital letter indicates that we are speaking of a divine, non-individualised nature or mind.

The spirit. This phrase is commonly used in a variety of ways. Your spirit describes that essence of you which is a spark of God, and which is eternal. Your spirit animates your soul. Sometimes the phrase, "the spirit of" something or someone is used somewhat casually when referring to the tangible essence of a seen or unseen being.

The spirit world. In our way, we refer to the etheric world or etherea. When a person or animal dies and the soul transitions from this earthly existence to the next sphere of experience, we commonly say that he or she has passed to the etheric world. It is not a place as we think of it but rather a sphere of consciousness. In our understanding there are many such "worlds," etherea being but one.

Those from the etheric world have described their environment and conditions in a variety of often contradictory ways. This is partly because, in the afterlife, we initially create the conditions we most need and which are different for everyone. But it is also because the impressions received from the etheric world must be filtered through the mind of the medium. For example, if a medium is firmly entrenched in Christian symbolism, he or she may speak in terms of heavenly gates and angels; a gardener may receive impressions in terms of flowers and plants. The intelligence of the etheric world is such that they will use the symbols most meaningful to the medium, and therefore those which will be most effective in communicating their thoughts.

Soul is animated by your spirit which is an aspect of the Great Spirit. Soul expresses itself through the filter of the incarnated vessel of body, mind and emotion.

The soul is a vehicle for the individualised expression of your spirit while upon the earth and survives death, but which is not eternal. Your soul has consciousness, native core energy, and layers of mental, emotional and physical attributes created by the soul's life experience.

An analogy we sometimes use is that of the glass blower. You might think of the glass blower as representative of the Creator and the molten liquid as the divine substance of all souls. That same material will take on different shapes depending upon how the glass blower turns the glass. Each vessel will be individual, but will have come from the same source. Each soul will have its own consciousness, but is forever connected to the Great Consciousness.

We all come from the same source and are equal; not the same, but equal.

The soul survives the event we call death, for a time, and it is the soul that communicates through the mind of a medium. Although aspects of personality and physicality fall away during the transformation we call death, these earthly attributes may still be given as evidence to the recipient in order to establish the identity of the spirit communicator.

Soul Formation

First, there was the thought.

The Creator's creation of that spark of the Divine, your soul, was first manifest in thought. Thus, the formation of your soul was conceived before physical conception.

In the realms of formation, your soul was bestowed with the conditions needed for its enlightenment and for the fulfilment of its destiny. Genetics, culture, time and place, biology, environment, family and so forth, were all decided before the spirit met that vessel which was to be your incarnation on the earth.

Once incarnate, we then began our return journey back toward our Beauty, toward the Divine Source, living out the fulfilment of our enlightenment through our soul's expression. The calling of your spirit ignited a *quickening of the soul*, to use an expression in the old way, an awakening to your spiritual nature.

Anything that forms cannot be eternal. Therefore the soul is not eternal, being formed prior to birth. That said, our soul survives the transition we call death and carries intact all the qualities that make us "us." However, at some far-off point after death, the spirit will no longer need this vehicle of the soul. The soul will then be shed when it has fulfilled its purpose, and when love has reunited us with those who have gone before. Love waits.

If you like, think of the cells of the physical body. Each cell has its unique cycle of life which, when it has accomplished its task, is replaced by the next cell to ensure the continuity of life itself. Such is the wondrous working of the Creator.

And so it is with the soul. For as long as we identify with soul we shall be within soul; once we no longer have a need for this vehicle, we let it go. Our present animal consciousness might be fearful at the thought of this "second death." But in time, the ever-expansive awareness of your spirit finds that it no longer needs to maintain aspects of its etheric body and moves on to a new way of being.

Not everyone is called to enlightenment in the same way. Depending on the level of spiritual awareness, the path taken is different for each and every one of us, both in the seen and the unseen worlds. There is no better than, there is no less than. In our way, all are equal.

When we speak of a soul's manifestation as being within the mineral, vegetable, animal and human conditions, we do not mean it in the sense of higher or lower states of being, but rather as an awareness of the parameters of our individual destinies. An understanding of the qualities associated with each of these conditions gives the medium a valuable insight into the nature of the soul formation of the individual with whom he or she is working.

For the present, let us simply be aware that a truly spiritual life is one lived with honesty, accepting that your soul was manifest upon this earth with divine intention. Every soul matters.

Psychism and Mediumship

We can never again profess ignorance of something once we are aware of it. This applies most especially to the spiritual laws that underpin the practice of mediumship.

Transcommunication is a sacred faculty. It is a sacred faculty because, using God-given abilities, a medium heals, inspires and becomes the voice of those who cannot speak for themselves. A medium is a sacred servant.

Above all else, mediums are here to serve those in the afterlife. They are the priority. The ethical responsibility to serve well and honestly can never be understated for, rest assured, every medium will one day come face-to-face with all those for whom they have been the intermediary. They will be held accountable to those whose words might have been deliberately withheld or misrepresented. This is not to say that honest mistakes won't be made, for this is to be expected as the medium gains experience in this highly complex art. Error is a very different thing than deception, however.

Spiritually speaking, we live the effect of our actions in eternity and so it behooves us to work with the purest of intentions and with the utmost honesty and integrity.

The development of our intuitive abilities, when properly nurtured, brings with it a heightened spiritual awareness. With increased awareness comes greater responsibility, a recognition of the influence we exercise for the upliftment of humanity, both here and hereafter. We have, above all, a responsibility to the One and to those in ethèrea whom we serve.

When we develop properly, sitting in the Presence naturally amplifies our emanation and hence, the effect of every thought, word and deed is amplified in proportion. Our impact as healers is magnified, both in work and in everyday life. On the other hand, we cannot afford to harbour negativity because of the magnified impact that it has upon ourself and others.

Working correctly within the Presence can actually help us come into balance when we choose to allow the inner healing to take its course. As our sensitivity increases, we need to do all we can to maintain and enhance that balance and to make the adjustments needed should we find ourselves, for instance, over-reacting or displaying diva-like behaviour! The more we develop, the more necessary it becomes to maintain a spiritual, physical, emotional and ethical equilibrium, both for our own sake and for the sake of the many worlds of creation.

And so, with this understanding of the spiritual implications of this work, of its ethical intention and responsibility, we shall now explore the particular fabric of the intuitive arts themselves.

What are the faculties we possess?

Instinct

Instinct is shared by all creatures of the animal kingdom. When we respond to the basic needs of the vessel, or when we react to outside stimuli in fear or pleasure, we are using our instinct. A case in point is the fight-or-flight response that resides within all creatures. If we have a leaning toward a particular talent, we may speak of "having an instinct" for something. Instinct is a faculty we all possess and use, simply by virtue of being a human animal.

Intuition

Yogananda taught that blind belief is not enough. We must have the experience of truth. "Intuition", he said, "is the soul's power of knowing God."[2]

Intuition is the soul speaking. Intuition arises when we have a "gut feeling" about something. We all possess intuition. Some are perhaps more trusting of their intuitive experience than others and use it more often. The sensate practitioner is one of these. The best exponent of any occupation, whether doctor or psychologist, tradesperson or athlete, is one who uses both their acquired craft and their intuition in harmonious cooperation.

Psychism

Psychism is the ability to perceive information from the vibration and aura of an incarnate source. In a psychic reading, the practitioner gathers information directly from the being or object in front of him or her. There is typically no contact with etheric beings when working on a purely psychic level.

Psychism, practised properly, is a spiritual act during which, as we used to say, we perceive the "delineations of the soul." It is a highly prized and valuable art. Whether we are sitting for an incarnate or a discarnate soul is of no consequence. We must always expect the same ethical degree of skill, compassion and sensitivity.

Every being or object that lives or has had a physical existence carries an energy which contains all the information about it. Many cultures and religious factions, for example, place great value on ashes and relics because they carry the residual energy of what was the essence of that being.

The depth of information received psychically is only limited by the ability of the intuitive. A good psychic may touch an object and be able to tell you where it came from, who made it, how old it is and so on. This is called *psychometry*. A proficient psychic diagnostician would be able to read the vibration and aura of blood, tissue and bone, and the memory contained within these. Remember, every living thing has consciousness, including each cell in the body.

There are a variety of psychic practices in addition to auric readings. Tarot, palmistry, astrology, numerology and other practices are rich, complex fields of study, each with its unique techniques and linked by some common mystical threads. Those who already practise mediumship may find a specialised secondary interest in one or more of these intuitive arts. In other instances, the exploration of one of these psychic practices may be used to trigger the potential intuitive faculty in a sensate individual.

Again, the successful use of each method depends upon the level of intuitive ability and the discipline of the practitioner.

Mediumship

From a purely technical standpoint, mediumship or transcommunication is the ability to perceive information from the vibration and mind of a discarnate source. When approached in the spirit of service, transcommunication is ultimately a healing modality.

Most of the mediumship practised today is mental, as opposed to physical mediumship. Depending upon the medium's biology, nature and training, impressions from a discarnate spirit are perceived by the mind in a variety of ways. Our psychic senses, being functions of the mind, are the translators of the impressions we receive. Although some mediums may objectively "see" a spirit form, most see subjectively. The manner in which they receive impressions may be commonly described in the following ways: clairsentience, to feel and sense clearly; clairvoyance, to see clearly; clairaudience, to hear clearly; claircognizance, to understand something to be true without use of the preceding three senses.

In addition to these fundamental avenues, some mediums may work in varying degrees of altered levels of consciousness, commonly known as trance. Healers are also mediums. A healing medium, inspirational speaker or inspirational writer, for example, will allow themselves to blend with the etheric world in order to receive influences from the discarnate source, thereby becoming the vehicle of communication. This is sometimes erroneously called "channeling."

Physical Mediumship

Physical phenomena are primarily the actions of the invisible becoming seen, felt or heard.

The great inspirer, Emma Hardinge Britten, once observed that, although one in seven people potentially possessed the faculty of mental mediumship, of that number only one in one hundred thousand possessed the ability to generate physical phenomena. This cannot be proven, of course, but it is cause to question any sudden proliferation of physical mediumship, as happens from time to time.

Nonetheless, physical phenomena do occur as they have in all cultures and throughout all the ages. Our fascination with the phenomena can be explained this way; it is an aspect of the God Mind made tangible.

Every great religion, every great spiritual path began with some form of phenomena. Often it was a physical phenomenon, meaning that it was seen or heard by many people at once. Physical phenomena are fundamentally the condensation of energy into matter and can take a variety of forms:

> *Percussion*: Audible noises, such as raps and knocks, that can be heard by all those within range.
>
> *Direct or Independent Voice:* The creation of an object that mimics the human voicebox, thus enabling the discarnate being to speak and be heard by all those present.
>
> *Materialisation:* The ability of the discarnate being to fully form in this world using ectoplasm, and therefore be seen by all those present. Ectoplasm is the out-of-the-body condensation of energy derived from those within the etheric world.
>
> *Psychoplasm* or *teleplasm* is the condensation of energy derived from the medium's mind.

Transfiguration: The formation of an ectoplasmic mask near the face of the physical medium, enabling a discarnate being to impress an image of themselves onto the mask and be seen by all those present.

Levitation: Objects or persons suspended or moving in mid-air without visible means of physical support.

Apport and asport: The relocation of an object from one place to another, or the appearance of an object from an unknown location, without apparent or visible means.

With the curious rise of so-called physical phenomena in our century, we are reminded of a time when the honourable spiritualistic tradition of physical mediumship fell into disrepute with the emergence of "dark seances" or seances held in unlit rooms. Obviously, the dangers of fraud are very real under such circumstances.

However, the etheric world makes no demand for such conditions. Emma Hardinge Britten wrote, "The fact that many of the most stupendous evidences of spirit power have been given in semi-lighted apartments should be a sufficient answer to those who plead for darkness as a necessary condition for strong demonstrations. Let dark circles be abandoned… and the impostors will find much of their occupation gone."[3]

Common sense for an uncommon practice.

King Midas

It happened that King Midas, in recognition of a great service performed for the god, Dionysus, was rewarded with the granting of a wish. Midas asked that whatever he touched should be turned into gold, and so it was bestowed. Overjoyed, Midas ordered a feast to be prepared, but every time he reached for food or drink it became inedible. Fearing starvation and realising his mistake, he begged Dionysus to reverse the cursed wish. His plea was heard. Understanding that gold will not feed a hungry man, King Midas withdrew from the royal court to the countryside and henceforth lived a life close to nature.

Desire

Chapter Seven:
Quality of Discernment

"It is not our bodies that think, but our spirits."

Emanuel Swedenborg[1]

Unbiased Perception

Subtlety within the art of transcommunication must be nurtured. It is nurtured to a great extent by the discipline, understanding and practice of the art of discernment. When working as we do with worlds unseen, unable to rely upon our physical senses for verification, we must develop that trust in our own ability to distinguish between perception and reality, between wish and need, between my feelings and yours.

First, we must be able to see clearly, for when discernment is clouded, healing cannot take place in either world.

Soul Imagination

Perhaps the question we are most often asked by novices is this: "How can I tell if what I am "getting" is merely the product of my imagination?" What they are really asking is, "Am I making this up or is it truly coming from a discarnate source? Am I fabricating with my mind or am I receiving impressions from elsewhere?" The ability to distinguish between the two is key to the honest development of the intuitive.

In our teaching, we impress upon our students the difference between mind imagination and soul imagination. Mind imagination is common to most of us. It is the natural ability to create images, sensations and ideas by means of our incarnate consciousness. It is consciously inventive. It is active.

Soul imagination, on the other hand, is linked to divine mind and is inspired by the collective consciousness. It is both a receptive and active state at the same time. The popular notion that you can *heal your life* through the power of thought cannot truly work because it is a function solely of the imagination of the mind. Real imagination comes from the soul. It is a faculty that needs to be nurtured and practised over time and one that, especially in the beginning, requires a most subtle discernment.

Core Energy

All living things, objects and locations possess what we ourselves have termed a "core energy", an inherent quality that remains constant throughout its existence. Over and above, around and through, and interwoven within this core are layer upon layer of energies that, in the case of a human being for example, reflect the ebb and flow of experiences, events, emotions, attitudes, actions, and so forth.

How do we think of this core energy? Let's use a somewhat oversimplified example. Think of the gold that is embedded in the earth as gold in its core energy. The accumulated energies of those who then mine it, transport it, cut it, shape it and finally create the gold ring become imprinted within its vibration; but the core nature of the gold remains the same, no matter what its final outward form.

The same applies to the core energy of an individual. It has a pulse, a resonance and a rhythm, whether we are speaking of a person, an object or a piece of land. It is not the emotional or mental state we seek here, as these are changeable. It is the core energy which, although subject to transformation and mutation, remains consistent in essence.

For the sensitive or medium, reading the core energy of something or someone requires that we remain a detached observer. We must strip everything away to find out what is really there in front of us, going beyond personality, beyond appearances, beyond our own view and perception to the very depths of our intuitive reception. It is not a thinking process but rather a psychic experience. We gather information psychically.

The ability to discern this core energy within all things is a fundamental psychic discipline. As a practising intuitive, recognition of our own core energy is essential, otherwise how can we hope to tell the difference between the outer reality and our inner subjective perception? This is, in fact, the first glimmerings of the discipleship of which we spoke earlier, that faculty of discernment which constitutes the beginning of the journey into the mediumistic consciousness.

An experiential understanding of the nature of this core energy is not easily acquired. It asks that we take a detached view beyond the five physical senses and come to experience this energy within our psychic senses. We are striving for pureness of thought in order to perceive this energy clearly. Once we find the core, we will then know the layers.

The core energy exists only as long as the being, object or location is incarnate. Although the innate quality and nature of the core energy does not alter, it may mutate or transform, and its strength may decrease over the life of its earthly incarnation.

Why do we need to recognise the core energy? Most people seek knowledge of themselves throughout their lives, either consciously or unconsciously. For many, the insight of a medium or a psychic is invaluable in revealing our essential nature, seeing difficult situations in a new light, and finding our way. Every mediumistic sitting is potentially a healing event.

In order to "see" another person with the impartial eyes of the spirit, a sensitive must be able to identify an individual's core energy as a platform of observation. Over and above this, we may then observe the ebb and flow of influences upon this person over time, as well as the active situations in which the person finds him or herself at the time of the sitting. Optimistically, we may then assume that the practitioner communicates these observations without colouring them with his or her own personal prejudice.

Although the lost art of intuitive diagnosis is less prevalent today than in earlier times and made even rarer for legal reasons, the knowledge of core energy is fundamental to the ability to discern when bone, tissue and cell are out of balance. Those who work with animals may receive information in a similar manner. A mother will consciously or unconsciously recognise the core energy of each of her children and be able to tell when "something is not right." Feng shui is a complex system of practices that employs this concept and is designed to establish optimum harmony in all areas of human life. Native cultures around the world have manifested their understanding of core energy in their art, ritual, and architecture.

Signature

Signature refers to the unique character and nature of the emanation created by an individual or group. It is sensed within the aura and is the most constant aspect of the soul. It might be likened to the spiritual counterpart of a handwritten signature.

The energy of a living creature has a distinctive rhythm that creates a pattern. This pattern is what we ourselves have termed the "signature".

Most of us have experienced a moment when someone we know well walks into a room and, although our back is turned and we cannot see them, we are able to sense who it is by their core energy, transmitted vibrationally through the aura. This is their signature.

For a host of reasons which become increasingly clear the more we work with this, it is important for a medium or psychic to be able to recognise a person's signature. It becomes a stable point of reference over and above which the practitioner can sense the layers and levels of the influences of the individual's life, whether they be of this world or the next.

Vibration and Aura

In the art of transcommunication, it is often difficult to find the words to fittingly describe the components of a non-physical, esoteric practice. The world of the spirit certainly cannot be defined by any earthly vocabulary and the invisible realms of psychism seem to defy our attempts to pinpoint their mysteries.

With this in mind, we shall nevertheless approach the concepts of vibration and aura, fully aware that they will only truly be understood when they are experienced.

What is vibration? Vibration, as we speak of it psychically, is a pattern of energy derived from spirit or matter. It is inherent in all physical and formerly physical things, and its frequency, intensity and character are a source of information for the psychic. The vibration emanating from someone's mental, emotional, physical and spiritual aspects contribute to the substance of the aura.

The core energies we spoke of previously each vibrate at a different frequency and thus, sensing the distinction between them, we can perceive their various natures.

Reading the core energy of a person can be likened to the scientific discovery of gravitational waves. These unseen waves ripple outwards into the universe from a body or event and carry information which cannot be detected by light, finally proving Einstein's theory of general relativity.

The ultra-sensitive instruments required to detect these gravitational waves somewhat mirror the psychic receptors of the sensate practitioner.

What is the aura? The aura comprises subtle fields of energy that surround, interpenetrate with, and emanate from a person or object; in one sense, a microcosm of the universal auric field emanated by the gravitational waves. The aura of a human being reflects who they are, what they think, how they feel and what their life experience has been. In short, the aura contains all of their data, physical, emotional, mental and spiritual. A practitioner uses his or her psychic abilities to gather information from the aura.

Contrary to popular belief, very few people actually see the aura objectively; that is to say, with their physical eyes. Most often an aura is sensed or felt. For instance, although some may see the colours of the aura with their physical eyes, most practitioners sense the vibration of each colour and are able to glean the information it carries.

The auric field is a kaleidoscope of colour and vibration. For the purposes of accurate discernment, however, we must first acknowledge the core energy, then move "upwards" to the vibrations created by the physical, mental and emotional bodies.

We need to be aware of the physical biology that created certain mental patterns which subsequently gave rise to specific emotional responses. That in itself is one limb of investigation with many branches. We constantly return to the awareness of the individual's core energy from which we may then follow yet another thread. We are not looking to uncover problems, but rather to discover the processes that reveal the true nature of the individual, thereby shedding some light for the recipient.

Once more we need to be on the alert to discern what information our own perception is giving us, and what is actually there. Where is this information coming from? Is our mind fabricating details or is our ability truly firing? This is the real work. Such discernment is the result of perseverance, patient practice and complete honesty with ourselves.

Indeed, sometimes the hardest part of becoming a medium is to let go of our long-held perceived truths.

This may be the time to correct a common misconception around the subject of the aura. There is nothing that can "infect" or "invade" the auric energy field. Neither is it vulnerable to rips and tears. These descriptions are simply the observer's interpretation of his or her perception of an aura. Auric damage is impossible.

The uncluttered, non-judgmental reading of an individual's aura will depend on the sensitive's power of observation, training and insight, and the degree to which their ability to read an aura has been honed.

Colour

Colour is one way in which we, as intuitives, perceive vibration. The faculty of working with colour is a major tool in our psychic repertoire. It is primarily used to read the aura of an incarnate or discarnate being with the intention, as always, of serving their need.

Colour is the reflection of a person's light, of their energy. The common misconception of a solid band of colour surrounding a body, designated with a fixed meaning, is far from the actuality. We, as human beings, are always in motion and so the auric field is constantly changing. That said, the colours of the core energy are relatively stable, but the layers over and above that can reveal a great deal about the physical, emotional, mental and spiritual aspects of a person at any given moment.

Not every intuitive sees colour objectively, or even subjectively. Most practitioners develop a means of sensing and feeling colour rather than seeing it. In our tradition, we ask the student to engage with each colour using all of the senses, not just sight. In this way the student becomes familiar with the wealth of information contained within the colour's rays, and uses all of their faculties to absorb its implications. This practice requires a freshness of mind and a willingness to trust in the impressions being received.

Historically speaking, certain colours may have specific associations, as they do in our tradition. Therefore, in addition to learning the colour concepts within the philosophy in which we are working, we encourage the student to develop a personal colour vocabulary. What do the colours mean to us? What feelings do they evoke?

As we build our own colour language, it is important to clearly identify our personal likes and dislikes, and to understand why they affect us in this way. Once our colour biases are known, their impact upon our judgment will be lessened. When we are no longer unconsciously swayed by the influence of our personal preferences, we are then free to be the observer and consequently able to interpret the true meaning of an auric colour without bias.

In the old way, the mediums used colour as a powerful healing tool. On a mundane level, we may also use it to enhance our own energies, choosing to wear a particular shade to augment our vitality, or selecting another to calm excited nerves in a stressful situation. Once we begin to expand our awareness of colour, we can use it consciously for our own well-being. For instance, renowned mediums Winifred Bentham and Fanny Higginson pinned particular colours to their undergarments when doing public demonstrations!

Colours are fluid, shaded and changeable within the auric field. A slight difference in shade, a variation in intensity, the location of the colour – all of these aspects must be considered in this complex and fascinating area of study that continually evolves over the working lifetime of a medium.

Symbol and Sign

Those who work within the intuitive arts are generally sensitive to symbol and sign as a means of guidance and communication.

Communication between whom? Obviously, the recipient is your mind or your soul. But who or where is the source?

Spiritually speaking, the origin of any significant symbol or sign is almost always to be found within the divine realm. We know that at the helm of all creation and manifestation is the Great Spirit reaching out to awaken your spirit. Symbols and signs are highly effective ways of doing so, if we are sufficiently awake to notice.

To those who put everything down to coincidence, we once again echo the words of Plotinus, "To make the existence and coherent structure of this Universe depend upon automatic activity and upon chance, is against all good sense."[2]

Synchronicity is a sign most of us pay attention to. For some intuitives it is an indication that they are "in the flow" or in tune with the rhythm of the spirit. For others, it is a reminder that God is present; a sign to awaken, to stay alert, to move.

It is important to point out here that not all the symbols and signs we identify are actually laden with meaning. That said, of course, everything in creation has relevance to us because it is an embodiment of the Great Spirit, and all Nature speaks to our soul of the magnificence of the Spirit body to which we belong. However, if in our neediness we attach importance to some eagerly wished-for sign, inventing moments of revelation when none exist outside of our desire for a certain outcome, then we must bring the power of reason to bear on our perceptions.

Once again, this subtle quality of discernment is enormously important to one moving toward the mediumistic consciousness. At no time, and in no circumstances, do we ever wish to create the *Emperor's New Clothes*.[3]

What is a symbol? A symbol represents something else. It usually has both literal and abstract associations and can evoke many things at one time. It more often calls us to contemplate than act, and encourages our mind to make associations.

Words, colours and icons are all symbols which may have universally common associations but represent different ideas in different cultures.

In Egyptian mythology, the Sun represents the god Ra; in the language of the tarot, vitality; in a kindergarten, a happy mood.

When a symbol emerges in mediumship it needs interpreting. Although some schools of psychic thought adhere to a common dictionary of symbols and their fixed meanings, we suggest that an intuitive may wish to develop his or her own intuitive vocabulary of symbols. The intelligence of the etheric world will embrace your symbolic language and access it for the purposes of communicating an idea that has relevance for the recipient. That said, in some instances, you may receive a sign or symbol from the etheric world which only the recipient will understand.

In our understanding, symbols already exist at some level. When a symbol is perceived, then understood, it becomes a sign; a sign to awaken, to respond or to move.

What is a sign? A sign means something to us. It gives us information. It usually calls us to action or guides us in a certain direction as we navigate our lives in this physical reality.

It may be a personal sign. For example, if you were told as a child that to find a penny on the pavement is good luck, any reoccurrence will likely imply that things look promising! Other signs may be more universally recognised. A human hand extended palm upwards is generally understood to be a sign asking for alms. When we see the *symbol* of a green sign showing a figure running through a doorway, it is a *sign* to us that we can exit at that location.

A significant sign received intuitively or mediumistically may originate with your archetypal self or with the etheric world, generating an impulse, a symbol for which is received by the medium's mind. It is assessed by intuition, then interpreted as a sign. Curiously, a sign is sometimes received repeatedly in various ways over a period of time, especially if we have chosen to ignore it the first time.

Before jumping to hopeful assumptions regarding the spiritual impli-cations of a symbol or sign, however, we need to ask, what is the intelligence behind it? Or, what is my subconscious trying to tell me? Or, what does the etheric world intend that I should understand? If you discern that it is simply a random event, let it be. If you can detect an intelligence behind the event and intuitively know its meaning, then acknowledge it gratefully.

As mediums on a spiritual path we always want to see what is *really* there, rather than what we wish to be there. Honesty in all things.

In esoteric mediumship, symbol and sign are inherent within the inner mysteries and constitute a hidden language of guidance and prophecy that is rich in ancient spiritual knowledge. Symbol and sign both reveal and conceal knowledge within mysticism. It is a vast, fascinating realm of study. However, one called Azur the Helper reminded us to keep all outward phenomena in balance: "Be ye not seekers for signs, but workers for the cause of the spirit of eternal truth."[4]

Cassandra and Apollo. (*Pitture d'Ercolano*, vol. ii. tav. 17.)

Apollo and Cassandra

The god Apollo fell in love with Cassandra, beautiful princess of Troy, and bestowed upon her the gift of prophecy. But Cassandra denied his advances and so he placed a curse upon her that, although she would see the future, no one would believe her prophecies. And thus her coveted gift brought her great despair.

When her countrymen found a gigantic wooden horse outside the gates of their city, Cassandra pleaded with them not to allow entry. She had foreseen that the Greeks would destroy them if they brought the horse into the city. No one believed her. The horse was admitted, and from within it emerged the Greek army which destroyed the great city of Troy. Blessed or cursed, adored or despised, the truth was spoken.

Moral Conscience

Chapter Eight:
Becoming a Balanced Medium

"Truth is the golden door of entrance to the human heart."

Andrew Jackson Davis[1]

Natural Ability

The pull to mediumship must come from within….

The true call to mediumship is spontaneous, natural and unforced. Both of our teachers, Winifred Bentham and Gordon Higginson, said that mediums are born not made, meaning that the ability must be there in the first place. It cannot be fabricated, only enhanced. Admittedly, one can be trained to accomplish certain psychic feats but this does not a medium make. Most people can be trained to play a tune on the piano but few are destined to be concert pianists.

In our way of training, the utmost care is paid to a balanced synchroni-sation between unfolding the student's natural ability and the acquisition of techniques. The one is never sacrificed for the other. For us, spiritual readiness is everything in the healthy unfolding of the medium. Unfortunately, some modern methods promote an overemphasis on the mechanics in isolation, leaving the student in an imprisoned state of magician consciousness which may eventually result in a kind of mediumistic dissociation.

As we work with a student of mediumship in the initial stages, their natural ability is purposefully aligned with basic techniques in order to establish a firm, balanced foundation. As the medium's ability then unfolds, that natural ability is encouraged to take precedence once again, potentially leading the way to the mystical consciousness.

This process can be likened to the classical training of an actor, wherein the natural talent is tempered temporarily in order to focus on the physical and vocal techniques that are the basis of the actor's craft. Once embedded, technique then takes a back seat as their innate ability is encouraged to come once again to the fore. This same process can be seen in other walks of life. A skilled auto mechanic who has a hunch about the source of a problem, or a baker who can tell exactly which conditions will produce the best pastry, have brought their original intuition into play once more after a period of practical apprenticeship.

The secret that is not a secret is to find one's passion; for to develop that talent whatever it may be, is to develop one's true spiritual nature.

Intention

As with any talent or ability, transcommunication can be used for the benefit of all or for the glorification of oneself. The significant difference between other disciplines and mediumship, however, is that the effects of our intentions are greatly amplified by virtue of the fact that we deal in energy. Our effect on the outer world and upon ourselves is far more impactful than it is for other arts and practices. Therefore, our responsibility is greater than for most.

In addition, if our intentions are ethical, as in the desire to serve, our ability will grow in fertile soil with unlimited access to nutrients; however, if the motivations are base, the ability itself will eventually founder and fade. It would be far better to pursue something that honestly gives us pleasure in the doing, whatever it may be, and to follow avenues that give full rein to our true talents and our spiritual nature.

Balance

Mediumship will not automatically make you more spiritual, nor will it necessarily bring you peace. If you are an unhappy or insecure person to begin with, the practice of mediumship will only magnify this or any other state.

This is because the whole premise of transcommunication is based upon developing your sensitivity, which also means a temporary shift of the mind to some extent in order to touch another reality.

It is paramount, therefore, that you are able to depend on your inner emotional and mental foundations, which are established through good training, ethical practice and compassionate intent. You must be able to recover your sense of stability at will. This is an integral part of our professional discipline. It is not an optional skill.

Attention to balance in daily life, including mental relaxation, grounding through physical activity and interaction with the material world in pleasurable, non-psychic ways are all essential to the development and maintenance of a healthy medium. We must always remember that our humanity is at the very core of compassionate practice.

Honesty

Whatever our level of ability and experience, honesty with ourselves and with others will permit the fullest expression of our talents. The whole medium settles for nothing less than the truth, to the extent of his or her awareness.

Where intuitive development is concerned, this is especially crucial because we are dealing with the delicate vehicle of the mind. When we train as mediums or sensitives, we are laying down pathways of thought patterns which, once established, are difficult to undo.

For instance, be grateful to the recipient who gives you an honest, resounding, "no" to a piece of evidence, for here is an opportunity to question the way in which we have received the information. Has it come from our own mind or have we perhaps misinterpreted the information received? Do we need to reword the statement for the recipient? Whatever the answer may be, you have been prevented from establishing an erroneous pattern of mind.

You will always develop your ability more strongly in the honest reality of who you are, rather than who you think you should be. Be the best "you" possible, in honesty and integrity. This may require considerable self-observation throughout your journey of development and practice. A willingness to change when change is needed, no matter the stage you find yourself at in your career, is crucial to your development. As Austrian philosopher, Rudolf Steiner put it, "In esoteric studies, everything depends on the energy, inward truthfulness and uncompromising sincerity with which we contemplate ourselves and our actions, from the standpoint of complete strangers."[2]

A good medium or sensitive chooses to be honest in every aspect of the work, without regard for saving face or displaying power. After all, it is not about us.

Adaptability

Truth itself does not change but our understanding of it alters. The practice of transcommunication changes with time because our understanding of it changes. If we hold fast to the proven methods of yesteryear and ignore the accumulated understanding of the age, we run the risk of hampering the opportunity to expand our range of service. A medium is ideally willing to adapt and to flex the mediumistic muscles along new avenues, provided that the new ways make sense.

We must also consider that, as our ability develops, the etheric world will find new ways to communicate and we must be open and ready.

Observation

An intuitive practitioner is a non-judgmental observer, an observer of self and others. In our training, observation is cultivated at every level, at first with a view to becoming aware of our own perceptions. In so doing, we come to recognise the filters we use to assess our world, heal them if need be, and thereby move toward becoming a truly holistic practitioner. This compassionate detachment is then woven into the fabric of our work with others, whether incarnate or discarnate. Consequently, we learn to distinguish with a fair degree of confidence between that which is our own perception and that which belongs to another.

As mediums and psychics, we are not here to judge, but to observe. This is paramount in our quest to become trustworthy servants to the etheric world and to our fellow human beings.

Perception and Pattern

The basic human capacity to perceive information is accomplished by means of the five physical senses, and also by means of the intuitive or psychic senses. Perception is our only means of making sense of the world, and therefore of exchanging impressions with each other or with the etheric world. We all share in this process, psychic or not, mystic or novice.

Our assessment of people and situations is largely the result of the view created by our life's experiences. This perceptive pattern is established through repetition over time. Our friends and family can usually predict our responses based on these patterns, even our *un*-predictability.

From the moment of birth our minds seek pattern. The primary function is to keep us safe. Through trial and error, we discover which actions create the results in the outside world that we think we need to ensure our physical and emotional survival. We create patterns of the mind.

As we age we continue to create and recreate those patterns which we believe will ensure our security, without calculating whether they are healthy or unhealthy, happy or unhappy, constructive or destructive. Our only desire is to feel safe. Thus, from our patterns we create a web of conclusions and perceptions which may remain largely unconscious. When these patterns of perception go unrecognised within ourselves as mediums, it significantly inhibits our potential.

In everyday life, our patterns of mind, likes and dislikes, fears and prejudices, and moral judgments all influence our responses to the people and the world around us. We who work within the mediumistic consciousness, however, must make deliberate attempts to acknowledge personal perceptions, then move beyond them in order to approach, as nearly as we possibly can, a state of psychic impartiality.

We strive to see past our subjective interpretation of things. A medium cannot afford to judge based upon personal notions of what is good or bad, moral or immoral, socially acceptable or not. In recognising our own perceptive patterns, we as mediums are then able to touch the *real* need of the spirit of the individual in front of us, rather than the perceived need.

Again, we must see what is really there, not what we think is there.

Sitting for the Presence of the Spirit

Sitting for the presence of the Spirit is the single most valuable practice in the development of transcommunication or any other aspect of spiritual work. It is the act of attunement with the Spirit, the God of Your Own Understanding, the Infinite Intelligence, or whatever words you use to speak of the source of all power. When we sit within the Presence we are blending with the Spirit, letting go of mundane concerns and opening our minds and hearts to an awareness of the presence of God.

You cannot be where the Presence is not. You cannot be where God is not. You may simply not be *aware* of it, just as a fish is not aware of the water it inhabits. The Presence of the Spirit is always there. It is a matter of bringing our focus to it. The more we become aware of the constant presence of the God-power, the more we develop a natural awareness of it in our daily lives. The intention of sitting for the Presence is to bring our attention to that natural ability of blending with the God Mind.

It is within this seemingly passive practice that our spiritual nature unfolds, our ability to hold the power expands, and our intuitive antennae begin to reach further afield under the influence of the Great Spirit. The 17th century Carmelite monk, Brother Lawrence, called it the "practice of the presence of God"[3], for it is a discipleship.

For mediums within our tradition, this is a daily and reverent practice. As we move to a place where we can be continually conscious of the God Presence, our healing ability is amplified and our sensitivity increases over time. Within this receptive state of alertness, we make ourselves available for service, trusting in the God of Our Own Understanding to unfold us in the way that is needed.

In times gone by, community members convened week after week and year after year, to sit together with no other motive than that of experiencing the joy of being in the presence of Spirit and listening to the voice of the spirit world. A resurgence of such patient practice would not be unwelcome today.

Sitting for the presence of the Spirit also refers to sitting in the God-power for the purpose of *listening* to the etheric world. It is not a question of "talking" to the discarnate being, but rather allowing them to manifest their intelligence in *their* way. It also affords us the great opportunity to be inspired by their wisdom, to develop our sensitivity, to receive communications of love, and to enjoy the tremendous privilege of simply being in their presence.

Once again, sitting for the presence of the Spirit is not a single act, but a lifelong practice of communion. In doing so, we surrender our innermost selves to the work of the Divine.

Natural Mediumship

The 20th century saw the establishment of the first schools of psychism and mediumship. Classes, workshops, and exercises designed to train mediums are a relatively recent phenomenon. A staggering vocabulary of structured development exercises, theory, methods and techniques has become as widely available to those serious in their intention to develop properly as to those with merely a passing curiosity.

Prior to this, knowledge was passed down from teacher to student in an oral tradition, and ability was nurtured by sitting with experienced mediums over a long period of time. One sat without necessarily expectation of manifestation, simply listening to the voice of the etheric world and bathing in the experience of the essence of the Presence.

In this way, you unfolded at the right time and in harmony with your soul's readiness. One sat regularly for the presence of the Spirit to allow for that same natural, integrated and reverent process which ultimately bestowed upon the world those great mystics, mediums and teachers throughout the ages. We ourselves were trained in this way – that is, to be "natural mediums." In our decades of experience as teachers, we know this to be still the best way.

The development of a medium lasts a lifetime. It must be understood that a medium has never arrived. However, from a purely mechanical point of view, we may safely estimate that a student will work for a period of ten years within the magician stage of development. It may vary depending upon factors that act as accelerants or brakes, such as personal growth, self-healing, opportunity, motivation and discipline. Some may already be working publicly with their mediumship during this period of apprenticeship and, over time, may often come to an awareness of "something missing" in their practice. Many then choose to return to their training in order to move forward, not necessarily in the mechanical sense, but toward the consciousness of the mystic.

Just as in days gone by, the unfoldment of your mediumship will ideally take place in balanced proportion with the unfoldment of your mind, however long that takes and at whatever chronological age you begin. You need healthy teachers, experienced and knowledgeable in both the spiritual and technical aspects, and a community of like-minded individuals who together can create an atmosphere of safety and harmony in which to work on a regular basis. Community is important, even if, to begin with, you number only a few like-minded members. Just as individually you lay down pathways of the mind, so does the collective mind lay down pathways for the spirit.

The Long Run

It is not uncommon these days to see people eager to become mediums and psychics participating in a workshop one week and drawing up their business plans the next. Frankly speaking, the motivation in such cases is generally ego-based or monetary. If this is the case, then one must certainly be honest with that.

In our tradition, however, this has little or nothing to do with the vital and sacred nature of transcommunication.

The work of the medium is lifelong. It stems from a soul-inspired impetus to be a vessel of divine service. In order to become a fit instrument for the etheric world, and for the Infinite Intelligence behind that, the true medium understands and accepts that the cultivation of his or her whole being is required. This is the discipleship essential to those who genuinely pursue the mediumistic consciousness.

It is a path not suited to the many, but rather to the few who are willing to commit, to make the sacrifices, to do the work, to tailor their lives to the needs of the spirit, and to demonstrate patience, discipline and compassion, asking for little more than the opportunity to serve well. It is not easy. It is not for everyone. You must be in it for the long run, not only within this existence, but the next and the next.

Pygmalion and Galatea

Pygmalion was a Greek sculptor of great talent who, though he disdained all women, was inspired to create the ideal woman out of marble. When his chisel finally stopped ringing, there stood before him a woman of such perfection that Pygmalion fell deeply in love. He called her Galatea. What irony that he who had scorned women should fall in love with one who could never love him in return!

In his agony, Pygmalion prayed to Aphrodite, Goddess of Love. She took pity on him and brought Galatea to life. The couple were wed and, ever after, Pygmalion paid grateful homage to Aphrodite for the great gift she had given him.

Divine Love

Chapter Nine:
Toward Your Beauty

"Let each man think himself an act of God,
His mind a thought, his life a breath of God;
And let each try, by great thoughts and good deeds,
To show the most of heaven he hath in him."

Philip James Bailey[1]

What is Your Beauty?

We have called this book *A Mediumistic Path to a Spiritual Life.*

Mediumship, when properly understood, is ultimately about becoming whole through the transformation of self. This transformation is at once mental, emotional, physical and spiritual, and guides us toward the revelation of our Beauty, a transformation which may also be called healing.

"Being is desirable because it is identical with Beauty, and Beauty is loved because it is Being." These are the words of the ancient philosopher, Plotinus, one from our lineage, speaking to us more than two thousand years ago. "We ourselves possess Beauty", he says, "when we are true to our own being... knowing ourselves, we are beautiful; in self-ignorance, we are ugly."[2]

Your Beauty is who you really are. It is the soul in its perfection. Your Beauty is the being behind the human mask, that mask of personality and habit whose construction began at the moment of earthly birth.

Your soul is formed prior to conception. Your physical makeup, family, culture and challenges are preordained by your spirit in order to create the conditions most suitable for unfoldment throughout your earthly life. Our physical attributes are the filter through which the soul perceives its environment. Your soul is aware of certain givens that await you in this incarnation, an awareness that usually recedes once earthly life commences.

At the moment of a newborn's first breath, the soul is in a perfect state of natural being. We say that it is *in its Beauty*, as close as it can be to the spiritual nature bestowed upon it by the Great Spirit.

In accordance with Divine Intelligence, this world is the rarified atmosphere in which our spirit experiences that thing called Life. The very nature of physical existence brings about seeming separation from our divine nature, from the Beauty which was our birthright.

Some of us may, at some time during the course of our lives, feel that pull back to the self, back to the Beauty that is our divine heritage. This is our spirit calling. It is a call to heal all of that which took us away from our nature. Remarkably, we somehow seem to know our way back home. The path is often familiar, though we cannot say why. For many, this longing leads us to the unfoldment of our innate talents which are an expression of who we really are. It is a path which turns us back upon that return journey to our Beauty, our nature and the revelation of who we truly are.

But how did we stray from our nature in the first place? In order to answer the basic instinct for physical survival, to satisfy our needs for sustenance, love, belonging, knowledge and power, we had to manipulate the elements and the people in our world. We therefore developed patterns of behaviour, personality and attitude to obtain the results we needed to survive and to ensure our safety, comfort and pleasure throughout life. Consequently, we may continue to see the world through these filters, even beyond their usefulness.

Your true Beauty lies beyond these patterns. Your Beauty goes beyond acquired personality, physical appearance, mental capacity or emotional makeup; beyond your prejudice, moral judgment, opinion, attitude or preference; beyond your race, gender, sexual orientation, persona, religious belief or social condition.

Importance for the Medium

As mediums working with worlds within worlds, our own personal patterns can cloud our view. For example, if we are unaware of our personal filters, we may almost imperceptibly react to a spirit communication with either indifference or prejudice, with pleasure or distaste, with or without compassion; when in fact, the actual intention of the spirit communicator may be entirely outside the realm of our perceptive judgment.

Working in our Beauty, however, unmasked as it were, we begin to see the reality of what *is* rather than the illusion created by the filters of our patterns. We are more likely to act rather than react. As mediums we can then truly be of service to the real need that is often hidden behind the masks of those in this world or in the etheric world who come to us for assistance.

Why is it important? The very practice of mediumship awakens our spiritual nature. There is ever a gentle whisper of spiritual invitation to approach a reverent union with the Divine in the discovery of our Beauty, which is itself a reflection of the Divine Nature. In this way, we may perceive with the soul and thereby offer true service.

Some will listen and choose to follow, others will not.

As we work with our ability, there is an urge toward the revealing of our true nature. Faced with the need to become that honest vehicle of expression which the God Nature demands, no other option seems acceptable. It being an exceptionally challenging road, however, we cannot say that every intuitive practitioner chooses to take it. Still others are simply unaware of the crucial link between the need to heal themselves and becoming the healer.

How can we ignore our own spiritual health and still expect to offer healing to another? In the understanding of Oneness, we are all connected. The act of creating your own healing will affect those around you by your very emanation. Therefore, the closer you come to your Beauty, the greater will be the healing effect of your mediumship. It is a natural law of cause and effect and cannot be otherwise.

When we work in our Beauty, we work from a foundation of compassion rather than sympathy, from a basis of acceptance rather than judgment. We know with clarity when we are serving someone's need rather than their want. We impartially view the positive and the negative, the so-called good or bad, the dark and the light, with an equanimity untainted by the commonly prevailing morals or by our own prejudices. We call this soul perception.

It seems apparent that the very existence of the intuitive ability is an indication that we are meant to discover and exercise its true spiritual purpose. Having recognised its true purpose, we are bound to act within the integrity of our Beauty.

How do you get to your Beauty? Let us assume, then, that you see the connection between your Beauty and your sacred purpose as a medium. Then there needs to be the willingness to undertake the work, together with an openness to change where change is needed.

There are, among our deep-seated patterns, some which interfere with our task as mediums. In pursuit of our Beauty, we work to dampen these down and overlay them with other pathways more suited to our spiritual duty, which is to work without bias of any kind. We often describe this process to our students as "calming the elephant," for some patterns are powerful indeed.

A lifetime of habits, patterns, defences, and survival skills is deeply embedded within the cells of our being. "Give me a child until he is seven and I will show you the man."[3] Aristotle is saying here that a child's patterns are indelibly imprinted during the first years of life and remain into adulthood. It is neither possible nor necessarily desirable to attempt to eradicate them. They were acquired for good reason and many have served a purpose to this point in our lives.

However, those of us on a spiritual path must be especially aware of any pattern which is unhealthy, or that causes us mental or emotional pain, and attempt to heal it. During the course of our lives such a pattern may be stirred into being again and again, especially when we feel threatened. Our task as mediums is to be awake to that trigger, look it squarely in the face, and then "put the elephant back to sleep."

For science clearly tells us that it is not possible to do away with our patterns completely. They will never leave the unconscious mind. What we can do, however, is calm them and overlay them with new pathways. In our tradition, we may access the archetype of the Warrior to guard against those things that trigger the old patterns. This is not something to be "achieved" but rather an ongoing awareness and ongoing work.

It is heartening to know that the process of transformation begins at some level the very instant it is sincerely welcomed. Once welcomed, you may find that opportunities present themselves which may challenge you, or invite you to step into the unfamiliar. For instance, among the Triads we touch upon in the next chapter are to be found the Three Guides, those challenges created to further our progress toward enlightenment and the attainment of our Beauty. You may also be presented with unexpected opportunities to enrich, explore, and create new avenues for heretofore dormant talents, inviting you to overcome your fears and step into the unknown.

Many popular self-healing methods suggest that we can heal ourselves through visualisation and other mind-driven techniques. But imagination of the mind alone cannot heal. Real imagination comes from the soul.

This is where the work begins, where the adventure begins, and where it is invaluable to have around and about you a community of supporters who are truth speakers. For it can only be in complete honesty, with self and with others, that the unfoldment into Beauty can happen.

"How can I connect with my spirit?" you ask.

You are already connected. It is only your awareness which is wanting.

For connecting to your soul nature is as simple as being yourself.

Oedipus and the Sphinx

There once lived a terrible monster called the Sphinx, with the head of a woman, the wings of a griffin and the body of a lion. The Sphinx had been sent by the gods to punish the citizens of Thebes by posing a riddle to all who passed on the road into the city. Those who could not answer were killed by the Sphinx.

The riddle was this: "What animal is that which in the morning goes on four feet, at noon on two, and in the evening upon three?" Oedipus ended the reign of terror by solving the riddle: "Man, who in childhood creeps on hands and knees, in manhood walks erect, and in old age with the aid of a staff."

The Sphinx cast herself from the rock, the siege ended and the grateful people of Thebes made Oedipus their king.

Understanding

Chapter Ten:
The Triads

"Love is the life of man. Wisdom is the light in which love sees."

Emanuel Swedenborg[1]

Divine Contemplations

The Triads are a series of philosophical contemplations rooted in ancient tradition. Plotinus and Iamblicus, among others within our theurgic lineage, expressed their philosophy within Triads as they sought to achieve oneness with the Divine through contemplation and ritual. In our way, the awareness that the Triads bring guides us toward the unfolding of our nature, our Beauty and our truth, and leads us back to the innate purity of the human soul which is our birthright.

The way of the medium on a pathway to the mystic is illumined by the teaching contained within each of the Triads. They lead us to discover the worlds within worlds of the universe. Such a pilgrimage begins with those working within the magician consciousness, with those inner world contemplations which then affect the outer world. The Triads awaken our understanding of the Divine and the divinity within us. They are rich in layers and levels of meaning and pertinent to us both in light of our personal spiritual progression in life and in view of our work as mediums.

Contemplation of the Triads focuses our hearts and our minds on the elements that make up our spiritual unfoldment as human beings. The Triads throw a spotlight on our patterns, on our strengths and our weaknesses. Consciously working with them in a practical way, though incredibly challenging, serves to bring us into a natural balance and strengthens the psyche of the intuitive. As the vessel is strengthened, so too is our ability to hold the power as mediums.

In our tradition, children are also encouraged to unfold their divine natures by considering some simple Triads such as *Iron, Silver, Gold.* Although we would no doubt use different word choices today, the moral substance is ageless: Iron represented evil for evil, silver represented good for good, and gold represented good for evil. Today we might say suffering for suffering, compassion for compassion, and compassion for suffering. As they find real examples of what this may look like to them in their everyday lives, it is intended to awaken them to a pathway in which they themselves may thrive naturally within the gold consciousness of the Divine. As the great mathematician and mystic, Pythagoras, once said, "Educate the children and it won't be necessary to punish the men."[2]

As teachers, we continually guide our serious students toward what we call their Soul Intelligence - that awakened state of awareness of unity in the One. It is the fruit of the patient, attentive attunement of their intuitive and psychic abilities. The Triads play an integral part in this process, anchoring their steps as they walk the sometimes unsteady ground that leads toward the unfoldment of their true natures. We teach the Triads in an intelligent sequence which purposefully deepens their personal, spiritual and mediumistic development. In this way, developing mediums are encouraged to develop their entire being and to see the world holistically.

The Triads spotlight those of our patterns that promote either pain or wellness and which, as we begin to understand them, may become tools of transformation in our quest for personal enlightenment. They highlight the illusion of our human perceptions and steer our spiritual view in the direction of Reality. They have everything to do with our soul expression as we strive to move transcommunication closer and closer to its proper place within the mystical experience.

The Triads are neither prayers nor mantras, and mere thought will not get us where we need to be. They demand action. They ask for change. They are a blueprint of discovery urging us on to contemplate their meaning for ourselves and to act upon those of our personal challenges which need healing in order to fulfill our true nature. A clear, strong and balanced human being makes for a clear, strong, and balanced medium.

There is no mastery here, only becoming.

For the sake of bringing the Triads closer to home, let us take three examples and touch briefly on the implications of each. As we do so, bear in mind that we are but skimming the surface for the moment, and that each Triad is intricate and multilayered, with profound ramifications for the medium and the mystic.

The Three Causes

Safety * Comfort * Pleasure

We are animal beings. Our actions and reactions are motivated by one or more of these basic causes: safety, comfort and pleasure.

Our physical survival as a species once depended upon instinct to keep us safe, telling us when to freeze, fight or fly in the face of danger. Once safe, our desire for comfort comes to the fore, sometimes prompted by the emotional desire to find that person or thing which, healthy or unhealthy, gives us at least the illusion of comfort. Then the mind seeks out things of pleasure to satisfy what we think are physical and emotional needs but which are, more than likely, simply wants.

The physical vessel of the animal is vulnerable to addiction. Whether we realise it or not, we are all addicted to something. Whether that be alcohol, drugs, food, relationships or a habit of some kind, we will continue to choose that addiction as long as it brings us the illusion of safety, comfort or pleasure. Change comes about when the substance or pattern no longer makes us feel safe, comfortable or happy.

Why does a medium need to understand all this? The answer is, in order to escape the bondage that addiction creates around our ability. Once we can see how we ourselves function according to these causes, we have the opportunity to do the work required to detach from them and thereby liberate our ability from the cloudy personal filters which inhibit that very clarity of sight we seek as mediums and mystics.

"In the land of the blind, the medium has one eye open."

Simon James

The Three Guides

Bodily Ills * Worldly Misfortune * Indiscriminate Loathing

Each of us reading these words has suffered one or more of these three events. Ill health and injury invariably strike us all at some time or another. The loss of loved ones or the loss of material possessions are fairly predictable events in the course of a lifetime. Most of us have experienced self-condemnation, or have been on the receiving end of a sharp tongue or harsh treatment without knowing why; indiscriminately, as it were, because the pain inflicted appears to be unwarranted.

Pain is part of life's pathway of spiritual transformation. The experience of suffering brings us the opportunity to heal and to progress from healing to knowledge, from knowledge to insight, and from insight to wisdom. We have the choice to heal the experience which, when transformed, may become wisdom. The true medium takes that wisdom and uses it to heal humanity.

And so we do not ask, "Why is God punishing me?" but rather, "What is the thought behind this suffering?" An experienced medium understands that the bigger picture behind the pain may reveal a truth that remains hidden to the many. A great healer, for instance, knows when the needs of the soul are better served by the illness than the cure.

What we want to do is minimise the suffering and maximise the joy. In the aftermath of painful events, the way in which we respond to misfortune and loss is at the heart of whether or not we allow ourselves to transform through suffering. You may choose to take the blows onboard and to harbour them until they integrate themselves into your very nature, but this can only prolong the suffering. Or you may choose to accept the loss, be completely honest with the feelings that accompany the loss, seek to understand if possible, and ultimately be aware of the opportunity that has been afforded you to move closer to your Beauty.

To some extent, pain is inevitable but suffering is an option. To heal or not to heal… the choice is yours.

> *"Minimise the suffering and maximise the joy."*
>
> Brian Robertson

The Three Wills

Free Will * Soul Will * Divine Will

In this Triad, we observe the movement of our soul, its progression from the fettered will of our personal patterns toward the surrender of our will to that of the Divine Mind. We move from self-concern to Divine Will.

Free Will, or choice, is dictated by our patterns, those of which we spoke in the Three Causes. We act instinctively within our animal nature and therefore make choices designed to quell our neediness. Choices made in this way, from the imprisoned will, lead toward pain and away from our Beauty.

When we move into Soul Will, we act according to our true nature, acknowledging the freedom to respond to our soul's calling. We listen to our intuition. And as we trust, so are we then able to surrender to the Divine Will of the Spirit. We follow the flow that is the rhythm of the power of the Spirit. Needless to say, this is where the medium and mystic aspire to be.

> *"No matter who we are, we are blessed with the opportunity and free will to unfold the priceless spirit within."*

> Brian Robertson

The Oracle of Delphi

The Oracle of Delphi could see the future and could only tell the truth. One day, King Croesus of Lydia came to the Oracle to ask if he would win his battle with the Persians on the morrow. The priestess smiled and told him that a great king would destroy a mighty empire. That was exactly what Croesus had wanted to hear. Knowing that the priestess always told the truth, he went away happy, leaving many gifts for the Oracle behind him.

The next day, when he led his men into battle, the forces of Lydia were utterly defeated and King Croesus was killed. The Oracle had spoken true, but not the truth that King Croesus had heard.

Perception

Chapter Eleven:
Voice of the Soul

*"Let us hold ourselves in a quiet, reverent attitude
that we may better breathe forth the peace
which has come to our souls."*

Gordon Higginson[1]

Altered States

Altered states of consciousness, or trance, are woven into the ancient and modern mystical disciplines. The word trance comes from the Latin *transire* meaning "to go across."[2] Trance is part of a continuum of altered states of consciousness. In the very simplest of terms, as mediums we neutralise our human patterns of perception in order to permit an inner sight which is normally hidden from our view. This sometimes brings with it an expansive knowing which would not generally be accessible to our everyday mind.

The very mention of the word "trance" seems to inspire awe and wonder, particularly within the imaginations of those who may only have read of it in the more sensational gothic novel. Our fascination with it may be explained by the glimpse it affords of the enticing possibility that, just perhaps, there is more to us than we thought.

However, somewhere along the line, trance became publicly associated with the supernatural, implying something which operates outside of natural law. In actual fact, the trance state comprises varying degrees of awareness and is eminently natural, especially in its more familiar manifestations. For instance, psychic or not, we all slip into various altered states fairly frequently during the course of a normal day, sleep being the most obvious example and daydreaming a popular second. We alter our states of awareness every time we become totally absorbed in an activity we love and lose consciousness of time and space, and as children we slipped easily into and out of a world of make-believe. Artists create from yet another layer of altered consciousness, one which brings inspiration and illumination.

As mediums, in the state of consciousness we call trance, we are moving ourselves out of the way in order to allow the movement of the etheric world to work through us with as much liberty as possible, unhampered by our personality, patterns, preferences or inhibitions. In this way, the flow of etheric intelligence and of the Intelligence of the Great Spirit is unfettered and can consequently influence the heart and mind of the listening medium without being censored by our personal filters.

The act of moving into trance is rarely involuntary despite what the more sensationally minded may wish you to believe. To declare oneself an unwilling victim of a trance control is to both abdicate responsibility and imply a want of discipline. Neither does being a trance medium make someone in any way more spiritually advanced than any other worker for the spirit. As with the musician, it is not the violin which is significant but rather the music; in our case, not the medium but the spirit communication.

That said, perhaps our primary consideration should be, "Why trance at all?" It is worth noting that both Gordon Higginson and the eminent healer, Harry Edwards eventually abandoned trance healing as they found it to be no more effective than mediumistic healing in the normal state of consciousness.

We must ask ourselves, "Does the Divine Intelligence require that I develop the trance condition at this time? Is it necessary or is it simply what I want?" These are questions not asked often enough. If the motive is ego-driven, more often than not trance will not develop; rather, the person will see the emergence of an archetype or sub-personality which may then be falsely groomed so as to have the appearance of a spirit guide. If trance proves to be the most effective mode of communion and communication for a medium, and if it affords the discarnate being the greatest possible freedom of expression, then it is an ability which is indeed precious beyond compare. However, we wish to be clear that the spirit world neither authorises, initiates nor induces the trance state. That is the subtle domain of the God-power behind all transcommunication.

All mediumship, but particularly trance mediumship, arises from the subjugation of the individual will to the Will of the Spirit. Since ancient times, the purpose of trance mediumship has been a most sacred one, and in many cultures this is still true today. Historically, trance had immense practical and spiritual value for a tribe or clan as a method of bringing about prophecy, thus ensuring the survival and prosperity of the people. The guidance received from a trance medium was held in high esteem and the act itself regarded with due reverence.

Of recent times in the western world, we have witnessed an alarming surge of popularity around trance mediumship with no nobler purpose than to create a somewhat singular sensation, as it were. And yet, the intrinsic mystical nature of trance mediumship itself has not altered and it retains all the sacred potential for good that ever it had. The outcome depends upon our use of and regard for it.

On a purely practical note, it hardly seems necessary to point out that if entrancement does not significantly improve upon the quality of your existing work as a medium, then perhaps you should question its benefit in that regard; for the personal sacrifices required for the ethical development of a good trance medium are not inconsiderable.

On a spiritual level, there are those who pursue various levels of trance mediumship in order to deepen their own attunement with Spirit, who seek to allow Spirit to guide them along the path of their own soul. Working with aspects of trance may be a stepping stone toward wider spiritual illumination, as it moves in tandem with a person's soul growth. Entrancement, when reverently practised and properly understood, may enrich and deepen the natural abilities whether they be mediumistic, intellectual or creative.

Brian recalls his own introduction to trance mediumship. "When I was fifteen years old, I was invited to attend Winnifred Bentham's circle. Although I had always been greatly interested in all aspects of the spirit, I had no idea what was about to happen. So there I quietly sat, surrounded by experienced sitters. Then an elderly lady came into the room, sat down and proceeded to go into trance. Her control came through, welcomed everybody and then began to speak. I remember that, as the guide spoke, my hands seemed to quadruple in size. In fact, the guide addressed me directly, saying that I would feel the effect in my hands. They became huge. Then he said, 'Now we'll begin. Our guests have arrived.'

"The first person who came through was my grandfather, with whom I was very close and who had figured prominently in my childhood. He spoke in his native Scottish dialect, with his distinctive manner of speech and familiar intonation. He reminisced, spoke of family memories and then, to my great surprise and even greater discomfort, regaled everyone present with details of what I myself had recently been up to – all from a tiny eighty-year-old woman whose voice belonged unmistakably to my grandfather. That was my introduction to that extremely rare occurrence known as trance impersonation.

"From that time forward, I sat regularly in the circle for development. I witnessed Winnie's many trance impersonations, male and female, old and young, in an astonishing variety of accents and languages.

"Most touchingly, I heard those who were grieving speak directly with their loved ones once again, just as they had in life.

"When, some years later, it was decided that I must leave the circle to broaden my experience, I left under the impression that all trance mediums were as magnificent as Winnie. But in all my years of experience since that time, I have met very few mediums capable of true trance impersonation, let alone one of her calibre.

"An ability such as hers is rare. And yet, she herself made it abundantly clear that, unless the altered state vastly improved a person's ability to manifest the needs of the spirit world, there was little point in it."

Even in trance mediumship, the outcome of a trance communication can sometimes be coloured by the medium's own mind. It is public knowledge that, while in trance, a number of mediums, including the great Estelle Roberts and Maurice Barbanell, predicted that there would be no World War Two. They had just lived through the horrors of the first World War and it is highly probable that their minds recoiled from the possibility of living through yet another inferno.

Trance mediumship is a highly specialised ability toward which a person has an aptitude and which may be developed with great care and discipline. It requires not only a latent talent but a generosity of mind that will allow for its fruitful expression. As with any other form of mediumship, trance communication flows most freely through those who genuinely surrender in service to the spirit, leaving all self-concern at the door. A true trance medium heeds the voice which echoes from the ancient mystery schools, *"Thy will, not mine, be done…."*

We in our tradition teach our children that, "All are but parts of one stupendous whole, Whose body Nature is, and God the soul."[3] These words of Alexander Pope reflect perfectly the knowledge that we are all souls within the Universal Soul, united, interconnected and part of the Soul of All which animates all creation.

We sometimes hear students of mediumship say that they have had trance experiences in which, for example, they have written in languages not their own or spoken about subjects which are unfamiliar to them in a normal state. In most cases, what we are looking at here is an ability to tap into the Soul of All, those realms wherein all is known and which is accessible to those who have the ability to tune in.

For instance, if we take the illustration of radio frequencies, Einstein would tune in to the mathematics channel, Mozart to the music channel and a demonstrating medium to the departed loved ones channel; overly simplistic of course, but closer to the truth in most instances than the assumption of trance.

Inspiration received in this fashion should be just as highly prized as any information received in the trance state; for the realisation that the Great Oversoul, the repository of all knowledge, exists in reality for the good of all, is an awakening of tremendous wonderment.

Spirit Guides

And so we come to the much-disputed subject of spirit guides.

There are many degrees and qualities of entrancement, as we have already considered. Given the marvellous complexity of the human mind and of the unconscious, we must look squarely at the question of whether a spirit guide is a completely separate entity or whether it may be a manifestation of an unrecognised aspect of our archetypal selves or sub-personalities. Both instances undoubtedly exist. However, we will be the better medium for truthfully challenging our assumptions about the presence of spirit guides and seeking the reality in every instance.

It is beholden upon us to ask, "Is this guide actually a discarnate mind, a distinct and separate entity from myself?" If so, the intelligence of the etheric world will supply you with verification, just as it would for any other mediumistic contact. In the absence of such evidence it must be acknowledged that the mind is fully capable of creating a guide which, though it appears to be unconnected to ourselves, is conceivably the manifestation of an unrecognised aspect of our archetypal self.

It is food for thought to consider the story of Eileen Garrett, one of the 20th century's most brilliant and most investigated trance mediums. While in the altered state, the question was asked whether the personality speaking was an aspect of herself or a separate entity. The answer given was simply, "Yes."

It all has to do with honesty. We mustn't be afraid to look at all possible sources of any kind of manifestation. And in your desire for the truth you shall then find the fullest expression of the God Nature through you, in trance or out, with a guide or not. Besides, given the genuine intention to heal, are we not agreed that the communication itself is more important than the means by which it is received?

Let us assume due responsibility. As the great Spiritualist medium, inspirer and teacher, Gordon Higginson said, "We must learn to be aware of all life through our consciousness and our link with the super-consciousness. In this way we can think for ourselves and direct our life. We should not constantly seek the advice of spirit people. They accept their responsibilities and do not call upon spirits from another world to live their lives for them!"[4]

Guides, helpers, guardians, devas and archetypes. Each of these is an energetic system which has arisen out of a common human impulse to externalise spirit. These unique embodiments have emerged from different cultures and at different times throughout history. The illusion is that often these so-called beings, who seem capable of protecting, inspiring and communing with us while we inhabit this earthly plane, appear to be distinct and separate spiritual entities from ourselves.

One who attempts to teach mediumship within the magician consciousness may regrettably reinforce this illusion in the student, assigning a spirit guide to one person and a spiritual helper to another; for the magician has yet to begin the journey of healing. Without healing and the personal spiritual integration it brings, the magician will create separation between the Self and a person's inherently divine strength, inspiration and wisdom.

The original sense of wholeness into which we were all born is soon forgotten as we begin to engage with the outer world, and as we are taught throughout our lives to perceive separation as the reality. But the awakening consciousness of the medium is once again drawn to seek out that original sense of unity, of oneness both within and without. In doing so, the medium rediscovers the power of his or her own spiritual nature.

In our way, we encourage movement away from the consciousness that tells us that we need to create a wise guide who exists separately from our nature, toward the realisation that those archetypes which are sometimes considered guides are more often manifestations of our own souls. The more we integrate the archetypes back into our own nature, the more we move from magician to mystic.

Our task as mystics is truly a simple and profound one. Find the guide that is your own soul.

Dream Time

Everyone dreams. But for the true mystic, it is a reverent doorway that leads to the Creator.

Within our tradition, some dreams were understood as a way of communicating with the soul and of receiving inspiration from the gods. Dreams guided our personal growth and aided in the attainment of our enlightenment – that blending of our identity with the fount of all Being which is Consciousness itself. Which is God.

Dreams were venerated as a portal into the invisible realms of God. Our history bears witness to this in the stories passed down to us from the great mystics. Pythagoras, Socrates, Siddhartha Gautama, Isaac ben Samuel of Acre, to name a few, were proficient in the art of the dream. The legacy of their dreams has had a momentous influence on our human spiritual history, leaving in their wake the formation of great religious philosophies, infinitely wise counsel, vision and prophecy. Throughout history prophetic dreamers have predicted natural disasters, wars, lottery wins, political results, births and assassinations. Joan of Arc and Abraham Lincoln both predicted their own deaths in prophetic dreams, and by his own admission, the germ of Albert Einstein's *Theory of General Relativity* was generated within dream time.

Mediums from our tradition were and are trained in the art of dream. Symbols, words, objects, animals and humans appearing during dream time were recognised as tools within the prophetic state and were once commonly called visions. This particular training is extensive and calls for the exacting development of the art of discernment.

Unfortunately, western culture often dismisses dreaming as being a subjective phenomenon with no spiritual relevance for us. There is little understanding of the reality of the worlds which the dream inhabits. As trained mediums, should we choose to listen, trust and surrender, the influence of the prophetic dream upon the course of our lives can be potentially immense.

"During the early 90's," Brian recalls, "I was holding a demonstration and gave a communication to an Asian gentleman who attended the evening in the company of his fellow travellers from the East. I described a particular holy man to him in great detail which he emphatically acknowledged. I then concluded by saying that this holy man had been murdered, a statement which seemed to send shock waves throughout his entire group. I thought no more about this until, some months later, a sequence of events began to unfold with most unexpected political and personal implications.

"A student of mine called Anne had a dream. She dreamt that I was holding a class in her home, as I often did in those days. She had gone upstairs momentarily to retrieve an article and, glancing through the window, was astonished to see a procession of thousands of monks filing past her house, headed by one who was obviously their leader. Hurrying downstairs to tell me, she heard a knock at the door, and opened it to see the leader standing there. She invited him in where, quietly and unseen by anyone but Anne, he took his place immediately behind me as I continued to lecture to the class, unaware of his presence. Suddenly, another student, Rosemary, became aware of the monk and excitedly pointed him out to me. I turned to look... and so her dream ended.

"Anne shared her dream with me but, as neither of us had a sense of its meaning, we decided to approach Rosemary to see if she could shed any light on it. This happened to be a Thursday evening when we normally conducted a healing service for which Rosemary always arrived early. So Anne and I approached her with the story of Anne's dream. As we began to recount the events of the dream, an astonished Rosemary pulled from her purse a letter of invitation addressed to me which had arrived in her mailbox that very day.

"It was from the Asian gentleman for whom I had given a communication some months earlier. He had not known how to reach me but, synchronistically, happened to be an acquaintance of Rosemary's and he had written to me, through her. He requested my professional services as a medium in a matter of some religious and political urgency. I eventually did travel to Asia and worked extensively with the religious order concerned, assisting them in unravelling a mystery with some considerable political ramifications.

"My experiences during that period, both enlightening and disturbing, later had a profound and enduring effect upon the spiritual direction of both me personally, and upon our spiritual community. Had I not learned of the dream, had I not paid it heed, any such letter of invitation to travel, no matter how intriguing, would have been dismissed as unrealistic and financially foolhardy for me at that time in my life. However, the resonance of Anne's dream continues to affect, not only me, but those around me to this very day. Such is the power of the presence of the Spirit."

Spirit communication takes many forms. Those who pursue the art of transcommunication may find that their experience with dreams is greatly amplified during their development and they may well experience aspects of these types of dream:

Apparition Dream: Receiving the visual, sensory or aural impression of someone who has died.

Consciousness Dream: Concurrently dreaming of events that are actually taking place in waking life.

Collective Dreams: Two or more individuals having the same dream on the same night, and the dream has significance.

Telepathic Dreams: Connecting with another person's thoughts within dream time.

Omen Dreams: Forewarning of an event about to happen.

Divine Dream: The most transparent of spiritual dreams in which the mystic receives direct instructions or teachings.

Prophetic Dreams: Precognitive dreams which later become realised.

Dreams may be subconscious or of the spirit. The difference lies in their content. For instance, a subconscious dream weaves our self-centred concerns throughout its movement. A spiritual dream is not rooted in a personal story but rather in the soul. Such images are archetypal in nature and we must have an understanding of archetypes from our theurgic tradition in order to interpret the dream.

All consciousness begins with a dream. Consciousness exists purely as a perceptive essence. Mind and spirit are inarticulate. Through mediumistic training, this infinite consciousness is awakened and realised in the dream, that dance of the Creator. We are a dream within that Dream.

As the great 20th century Belgian artist, René Magritte once said, "If the dream is a translation of waking life, waking life is also a translation of the dream."[5]

The Myth of Halcyon

The goddess Halcyon was married to the mortal king, Ceyx. They shared a profound love for each other. One day Ceyx announced that he was to sail to Delphi to consult the Oracle. Halcyon, who was afraid of the sea, begged him not to go. But sail he did and his ship was lost in a storm along the coast.

In a dream, Halcyon received knowledge that Ceyx had been drowned, and when she found where his body had been washed ashore, she threw herself into the sea. The gods, moved by her devotion, turned them both into kingfishers so that they could continue their lives together, and gave them fourteen days of calm weather in mid-winter during which they could come ashore. These are the halcyon days.

Devotion

Chapter Twelve:
To Heal

*"Healing, no matter how spectacular, is not a miracle.
All cures are achieved within spiritual and natural laws."*

Tom Johanson[1]

The Act of Healing

Healing is the purpose of all forms of mediumship.

Some mediums are strongly drawn to the practice of mediumistic healing. They serve as a vessel for the power of the Presence which is the true source of the healing. A healing medium knows that he or she does not actually heal, because he or she does not control or direct the healing power. They allow the healing to come from Spirit, through their spirit, to touch the recipient in whichever way is needed.

Most healers, you will find, are among the most passionate of all mediums. The discipline required to become a healing medium can only be sustained by a dedication and compassion to see them through the many years required to become an instrument of service in this way.

When we heal, we manifest the invisible influence of Love. We are the conduits and the transformers of the God-power, from Divine Mind to the earthly body, from divine intention to its manifestation. It is unquestionably a calling, for the mind, body and soul of the healer must cooperate without reserve in complete surrender to the God Mind.

It has been our honour to advise a great many surgeons and medical practitioners over the years, many of whom sought training in the art of mediumistic healing and diagnostics. We invariably found that those with a heightened intuitive ability and who integrated this ability into their practice, were considered outstanding practitioners in their respective fields.

How does mediumistic healing differ from energetic healing? A great many so-called alternative therapies have resurfaced in the past century. Those therapies which fall within the realm of "energetic" healing appear, on the surface, to bear some similarity to mediumistic healing; however, this is not the case.

In the most simplistic terms, an energetic healer draws upon his or her own vital forces to effect a change in the recipient. A healing medium understands that he or she is not the source of healing, and is simply the instrument through which the Divine Presence may work.

An energetic healer generally works toward a specific result dictated by the apparent nature of the physical complaint or the mental distress of the recipient. A healing medium recognises that only the Divine Intelligence knows where healing is most needed by the spirit of the recipient, and allows the healing to flow without expectation of a specific outcome. It is a matter of surrendering to the Divine Intelligence.

When a practitioner experiences feelings of depletion or fatigue, this can sometimes be an indication that they are drawing upon their finite personal resources of energy to effect a result within the recipient. For a healing medium, this would be a reminder to get out of the way and to allow the greater power to have complete freedom to heal in the way that is most needed by the recipient.

How does one become a healing medium? The first prerequisite is a knowledge of the healing power of the Divine Intelligence, and the second, a deep compassion for humanity.

Then, as always, we look to our motives. Why do we want to become a healing medium? A natural healer has a genuine desire to aid in the well-being of another human being. That said, we also need to be wary that this natural desire to heal others is not the result of an unconscious wish to avoid healing our own "stuff."

The development of a healing medium is a lifelong discipline. In our tradition a healing medium prepares his or her own physical, emotional, mental and moral instrument in such a way as to become the most effective vessel for the work of the Spirit. It is not merely a question of acquiring healing techniques.

The first and most fundamental step must be to heal oneself, a stage which many would-be healers unfortunately bypass. It can be uncomfortable and difficult. But it is a healer's duty to prepare his or her whole vessel – mind, body and emotion – in order to become a clear and effective channel of the healing power. What would be the outcome if a surgeon performed an operation without first washing his own hands?

The work of a healing medium is largely facilitated by the faculty of attunement, or blending, which then initiates the flow of healing. The ability of the healing medium to hold this delicate balance of passive and active awareness is a matter of understanding, training, and then regular, thoughtful practice. A healing medium also understands how to initiate the three-fold process of intention, creation and manifestation, itself a profound discipline which we shall consider in another volume.

As healers, we are bound to guide our own personal moral and spiritual compass in our everyday lives. The thoughts we think, the actions we take, the way we live, and the way we choose to behave has everything to do with the ability we may or may not exercise as healing mediums.

In our tradition, when a healing medium sets to work, he or she does so with the sole intention of serving the spirit of the recipient. A healing medium knows that he or she is not the one who heals, and has no investment in the outcome despite the natural human wish to see a betterment in the condition for which healing was sought. When we call upon the Divine Presence for healing, we trust and know that the shift in condition within the recipient will be the one that is most needed for his or her spirit. This may well mean a physical improvement or a cure. It may not. It is not up to us. But healing at some level always takes place.

The outward results of a healing depend upon factors over which we, as healers, have no influence. For example, although a damaged limb may not be restored to full function as we envision it should, the Intelligence of the God Mind has directed the healing power to the area where it is most needed for the recipient's spiritual progress. This may indeed result in a physical healing; but it may equally affect an unseen aspect of the recipient.

Another consideration when assessing the apparent outcome of a healing may be the readiness or resistance of the recipient's spirit to being healed. The physical restoration of function and form to the body may or may not be ultimately beneficial to the recipient's soul progression. Again, this is a judgment we are not spiritually equipped to make.

Trust in the wisdom of Divine Intelligence requires more of us than simply wishing it so. Trust needs to be nurtured with both the head and the heart. The natural tendency of the human mind to harbour doubt may well lead us to wonder if healing is taking place. And yet we know and can feel that the power of the Presence is close and with this knowledge we, as healers, return again and again to our conscious practice. Faith gives rise to knowledge and knowledge gives rise to faith. It is within the very practice itself that trust in the action of the great healing power is built upon solid ground.

One in the Power, One in the Spirit

It has long been our daily practice to begin every healing session by sitting in the Presence, deepening our awareness of the Presence of God with the words, spoken or silent, *One in the Power, One in the Spirit.*

We are practitioners of theurgic healing which is divine in origin. It is divine because God works through the healer to touch the recipient, whether that be of mind, body, emotion or soul. It is a divine event for both healer and subject.

The words in themselves are not magic. The heightened state of being they evoke comes about through years of daily discipline, cultivating one's true nature and sitting regularly within the Presence.

Although the mysteries of theurgic healing are embedded within the Divine One, their effects come about only with disciplined practice. In brief, through work. There are no shortcuts.

Orpheus and Eurydice

Orpheus, son of the god Apollo, played the lyre with such perfection that every living thing was entranced by his music.

Orpheus fell in love and married the great beauty, Eurydice. They lived happily together until she was bitten by a snake and died. Upon the advice of Apollo, Orpheus descended to the Underworld and there played his lyre for the god, Hades, melting his cold heart. Hades told him that he might have Eurydice back again if he patiently allowed her to follow him from the dark into the light, but he must not look back at her or he would lose her forever.

Ascending from the darkness to the light, Orpheus could not hear Eurydice's footsteps behind him and began to doubt. He turned to look back. The shadow that was Eurydice was whisked back among the dead and lost to him forever.

Trust

Chapter Thirteen:
Death

*"The tomb is not a blind alley, it is a thoroughfare.
It closes on the twilight, it opens on the dawn."*

Victor Hugo[1]

Legacy of Death

Those of us who move within the mediumistic consciousness and who have been privileged to accompany someone on their final earthly journey may tell you that, in retrospect, death is a gift. Not, as some might think, simply because it is a release from pain or that a burden of responsibility has been lifted; but because death may stir up spiritual resonances within the hearts of those connected to the one who passes. It may move our soul awareness and shift our attention to the centre of our own being. If we allow it to be so.

Why do we grieve? We grieve because we experience separation. Separation from God causes suffering. And when we have experienced an aspect of spiritual oneness within a human relationship, we then experience suffering when that relationship ceases to be.

Regrettably, in our western culture, we have devised a myriad of inventive ways both to avoid feeling grief and to avoid thinking about what happens after we die. And so, we rob ourselves of being present during perhaps the most significant event in life – death. One who is awake will understand it as a window of revelation into the world that is our next port of call.

At the very least, the great message of a life lived becomes more clear to us after the person's death. As we reflect on the impact of someone's life upon our own, so we consciously or unconsciously either embrace or reject their influence upon us; this contemplation affects our future attitudes and actions. They leave for us their essence from which we may draw wisdom should we so choose. Such is their legacy.

Mediums are supremely aware that life continues after death. Even so, the pain of being "left behind" by the death of a loved one is no less profound for us than for the one who does not know. The sense of emptiness, of longing, of shock is the same. The difference is that when we know that death is far from being the final chapter, we may eventually begin to temper our grief and allow the transformation to begin. We may, over time, move from fear to awe, from dread to wonder, and be present to the divine experience which unfolds even in our long bereavement.

And above all, when we understand the majesty of death, and understand that our spirits continue in a manner reflective of our actions here on the earth, it gives this existence considerably more meaning, esteem and moral intensity.

The event called Death can be the very flame which ignites a passion for Life.

After Death

"By your light shall ye be known…"

When we pass to etherea we are seen for who we truly are. Nothing is hidden. It is only in this world that we attempt to hide. In the next world, our true nature is revealed. Would it not be a wonderful thing, then, to choose to be in our light here and now?

The masks we wear in this world are a construct of our personalities, devised over the years to cope with life circumstances or engage with others in our world. Personality is tied to our earthly life and, when we die, it remains a part of us until it is no longer needed. When we arrive in that new condition after the event we call death, we will be known solely by our essence, by our light.

Neither the mind nor the emotions are physical organs. They are not bound by matter and therefore they continue as patterns after death. When we die, the physical body falls away and we find ourselves inhabiting our soul. The soul carries with it the patterns of our personality, thoughts, emotions and identity. These attributes are not suddenly gone when we die.

The next world is not so much a place as a sphere of being. Since the mind within soul survives earthly death, the conditions in which we find ourselves immediately after death will be those most conducive to our immediate needs and expectations. In other words, what we need we create. As our awareness changes, so will our environment. This is why we hear so many different versions of what is to be found in the next world.

Fear of Death

The depth of fear surrounding death can usually be traced to its primal foundation – loss of identity. We fear that when we die "I" will cease to exist. Images of a black void may arise, together with a feeling of powerlessness to prevent our ultimate annihilation. No wonder death holds such terror, if this is our perception.

One within the mediumistic consciousness knows that death is but a passageway to yet another stage in a continuing life, and that your spirit always moves forward in eternal progress. If in doubt about this fact, there are volumes of historical evidence, mountains of scientifically researched phenomena, together with the invaluable work of present day mediums to prove to us, if indeed we need such proof, that we never die. Love, like life, continues. As the great Chinese philosopher, Lao Tzu said, "What the caterpillar calls the end, the rest of the world calls a butterfly."[2]

A Medium's Duty

One of the noblest and most significant services a medium can offer is that of healing, to facilitate a communication between those who grieve and their loved ones in the etheric world.

The grief-stricken who come to a medium in search of one more word from a departed loved one are in desperate need of hope that life continues, that the loved one is alright, and that they shall meet their loved one again. If the medium's work has been done well, a profound healing in both worlds may be set in motion, one that has unimaginable spiritual resonances.

Such a healing is most likely to take place when the mediumistic consciousness is sufficiently developed to allow the presence of the spirit to be felt. No matter how much detailed evidence is correctly given by the medium, healing at the soul level is most profound when the essence of the loved one is felt or recognised by the recipient. Though evidential verification is obviously needed, purely mechanical mediumship is less likely to create those rounded circumstances which create movement of the soul on both sides of the veil. It needs a whole medium to do that, one who has the mystical understanding needed to bring the essence of the loved one into the presence of the living.

Mediums communicate with the living, not the dead; for a being without a physical body is no less a being than you or me. The realisation that we shall one day meet all those whom we have served must surely inspire us to offer only the best of ourselves and our work in their service. Above all, the responsibility to represent them truthfully is a moral duty we must regard with reverence. Just as we would not appreciate someone putting words into our mouth in this life, so it is for those in spirit. We must take care to serve with integrity so as never to be in debt; for a debt must always be paid. At the very least, we owe them unblemished honesty.

As mediums, let us be as a mirror, reflecting the light of the one in the etheric world. Let us allow our abilities to function beyond the mechanics. Be within that space of the Spirit in order that we may bring the very Presence of God into our world.

In the Name of Compassion

May we speak for a moment to those of you who have suffered the loss of a loved one and are grieving, as well as to those practising mediums and teachers who are charged with their care and keeping.

We urge you to consider this: that the mediumistic development of those who are in a state of grief is an error of judgement that has the potential to do enormous harm to the soul of the mourner. We are aware that this is not necessarily the popular view; however, we must speak as we have found in our long experience.

Understandably, the one who grieves is often under the misapprehension that developing their mediumship will heal their pain, and that communicating with those in the afterlife is the magical key to their healing. This could not be further from the truth. Psychic development at such a time will only serve to distract them from their real personal healing, and will likely cause a further fracturing of the emotional self.

As teachers, our moral priority must be one of holistic healing. The spiritual peace and inner wholeness of those who grieve should be our sole aim - certainly not the development of their mediumistic ability regardless of their potential, or lack of it. This has absolutely nothing to do with it. The ultimate well-being of their soul does.

Let us always be mindful of our healing purpose as spiritual mediums.

Echo and Narcissus

A beautiful nymph called Echo fell in love with the handsome Narcissus. But, as she could only repeat sounds made by others, she could not tell him of her love. One day, she appeared to him but he cruelly rejected her. Shunned, she faded away leaving only the memory of her voice in the air. As she did so, a prayer was uttered that Narcissus might one day feel what it was to love and meet no return of affection.

It happened that, cooling himself by a pool one warm afternoon, Narcissus saw his reflection and, thinking it to be a water sprite, fell in love. Try as he might, Narcissus could not get the sprite to return his affections or speak to him. Narcissus became consumed, ceased to eat or drink, and gradually wasted away. Now, where he once lay by the pool, can be found the flower which bears his name.

Egotism

Chapter Fourteen:
For Your Contemplation

"The highest and richest inheritance is a truthful mind..."

Andrew Jackson Davis[1]

Contrasts

Most of us would agree that our earthly existence is about contrasts. Were we not familiar with sorrow, we would not appreciate joy in equal measure; someone who has never been ill may not fully appreciate the pleasure of wellness. Many such examples may occur to you.

Indeed, our very planetary system expresses itself in counterparts – light and dark, sun and moon, heat and cold, life and death, all demonstrating the ever-oscillating and rebalancing motion of nature which is never still.

It may seem that we are stating the obvious, which of course we are. We suggest, nevertheless, that here is yet another instance of one of life's mysteries hidden in plain sight.

Why cannot life be always beautiful? Why is there pain? What is the point? What kind of deity would allow mass atrocities to be committed upon this earth? Am I supposed to "learn" something from my pain?

In our lineage, the many Triads of which we spoke previously are a valuable means of focusing our hearts and minds upon these core matters. In doing so, we are able to expand our understanding without expectation of resolution. Likewise, we do not presume to provide you with answers to the great questions which have been posed since time immemorial, but rather to offer thoughts for your own contemplation.

And so, for the moment, we invite you to temporarily put aside your subjective patterns of judgment in order to consider the larger picture.

Suffering and Pleasure

Each of us is here on earth seeking our own enlightenment, whether that be consciously or unconsciously. The soul is awake even if the human sensibility is asleep. In other words, some may be highly aware of their spiritual quest for knowledge, while others may less intentionally achieve their enlightenment in other ways. We are all equal though our paths may be diverse.

One thing is certain, however; all of us will experience hardship at some point in our lives and therefore pain is inevitable. The extent of suffering, on the other hand, is in our own hands to some fair degree. It is within our capacity to temper its impact upon us. Suffering is the opportunity which was established in soul formation, the pre-determined circumstances by which our soul could most effectively come into its own.

The same applies to pleasure. We are naturally pleasure-seeking creatures. But is it not true that the intensity of our present pleasure is somewhat in proportion to the intensity of our past pain? Are not the pleasures of freedom immensely heightened for a prisoner of war, for example? And is not the pain of losing a loved one in proportion to the depth of our love for them?

As we go deeper, things can become even less well defined. For some, suffering is pleasurable. For others, pleasure is painful. Is this not so? A person who has been mistreated may unwittingly recreate those same conditions in future relationships because this is his or her concept of safety. A wealthy entrepreneur may repeatedly sabotage the pleasures of amassing a fortune if the belief of being undeserving runs deeply enough. How, then, can we state that pleasure is always good and pain is always bad? We create those circumstances in our life best suited to our spiritual development whether they are healthy or unhealthy, good or bad, pleasurable or painful, socially acceptable or not. Neither are we, in our limited earthly view, equipped to pass judgment on another's passage. Soul progression is open to all whatever the chosen path, and suffering and pleasure are merely two sides of the same coin of perception.

Contrary to popular belief, an event is not necessarily something from which we are meant to learn a lesson. Oftentimes it is simply an experience from which we can heal and thereby gain knowledge, which leads onwards to yet another experience and so forth, along the spiralling upward path of our soul's progression.

The mediumistic and mystic consciousness recognises that suffering is a doorway to transformation. The immature magician views it as a struggle, and he or she the victim. But suffering may be part of the pathway to the God of One's Own Understanding. The experience of suffering brings us to the opportunity of healing; and from healing to knowledge, from knowledge to experience, and from experience to wisdom on the spiritual path.

Natural Law and "Life Lessons"

The natural law of cause and effect is a supremely just one. When the wind blows, the tree compensates by bending so that it does not break. This is neither good nor bad, right nor wrong, nor a question of judgment. Compensation is simply a natural law, divine and inevitable.

And so it is with us.

For instance, when we serve another human being in need, that demonstration of love is healing for both parties. We do not create the healing. It is simply an outcome, a natural compensation of the divine law of cause and effect. Likewise, if we choose to ignore the calling of our own nature, we may find that our bodies sometimes compensate with physical imbalance or illness. It is not punishment. It is natural, inevitable counterbalance.

We are neither punished by an angry deity nor rewarded by a pleased one. But rather, our actions have consequences for which we are responsible. There are no special divine dispensations and no so-called miracles. There is simply the immutable, beautiful and eternal natural law of cause and effect.

We know that the choices we make have resonances as we move through life, to death, to life again. As Pythagoras said, "There is no word or action but has its echo in Eternity. Thought is an Idea in transit, which when once released, never can be lured back… all that thou thinkest, sayest, or doest bears perpetual record of itself, enduring for Eternity."[2]

As we awaken to the power of this principle, when we understand that what we say, think and do *always* creates a balancing outcome, we become free.

With freedom comes responsibility for our own actions, in the realisation that we ourselves have the means to effect inner change, thereby affecting the outer world. We have influence upon the quality of our eternal life going forward.

In today's jargon, when something unfortunate happens to us we are often reminded to think of it as a "life lesson," as though we are at the mercy of forces which purposefully come to wreak havoc upon us and thereby teach us something.

It is true that some life events may and ought to cause us to reflect upon the actions we have created in the past to effect an outcome.

Attempting to understand how and why we have created a recurring situation may reveal a hidden aspect of our own nature and thereby broaden our understanding.

It is also true that some events are just the stuff of life.

So how do we know the difference? There is no difference. It is not a matter of life lessons. It is a matter of experience. Experience intended, not to blame, but to *awaken* us to create movement toward the revelation of our true nature and our Beauty. The soul seeks enlightenment, but it must do so through the filter of the vessel which is the human animal. To assume that all experience is a divine life lesson is to not understand the human condition. We are animals. We sometimes act upon instinct and animalistic impulse. We are hardwired to create patterns that keep us safe, rarely calculating whether they are healthy or unhealthy for us. The blueberry shake that gave you heartburn was not a life lesson. It was an experience resulting from the choice of your animal nature. To avoid heartburn the next time, you may choose to resist the animal impulse and avoid the shake. Or not.

So not everything that happens in our lives is a life lesson choreographed by the Divine. If anything, it is about awareness. It is about awakening to the divine experience of being alive.

As we take stock of our life experiences, therefore, let us be sensible in every sense of that word.

Pattern and Beauty

We have referred repeatedly in this volume to your Beauty. Pattern is Beauty's counterpart. Let us explain.

When first you were born, you were as close as ever you will be to your Beauty while on this earth. It is who you were at first breath, an unadulterated soul embodied in a physical vessel. It is who you were before personality began to assert those characteristics devised for survival in this world. It is who you were before the motif of your earthly identity was shaped by the influence of the people and circumstances around you.

Beauty is where we want to be again. Its re-attainment is one of our spiritual goals. We may begin to find our way back to Beauty by looking at our patterns.

The discovery of our personal patterns takes courage, honesty and perseverance for it is a complex subject with a multitude of layers and levels. The Three Causes of Safety, Comfort and Pleasure are major contributors to the patterns we develop over a lifetime.

Our physical and mental survival depends upon our ego's recognition of what is safe for us and what is not. Whether this is true in reality is beside the point. The fact is, we believe it to be so. Repetition of subsequent behaviours and responses creates patterns within our psyche and we begin to see the world with a filtered view, through a glass darkly, as it were, interpreting all we perceive through that filter.

Why is this important for a practising sensitive to recognise? Because if we work with our patterns activated, we are assessing another person's reality with our restricted view and therefore cannot hope to see what is truly there for the recipient. In other words, we impose our own interpretation on the information received, usually without being aware of doing so.

Our task as mediums and mystics is to go beyond our patterns and into our Beauty. From this impartial standpoint we can then truly "see." Perfect vision is, of course, unattainable but the striving brings great rewards both for you and for all those whom you touch.

Solitude and Community

The path to enlightenment is a solitary one in the sense that it is we alone who do the daily work needed to fulfill our true potential. It is a solitary passage because no other human being can take either the blame or the credit for the outcome of our choices. Personal responsibility is a solo endeavour.

That said, the working out of our soul's progression is ideally done in the company of others. We only feel and see the results of our thinking and our actions as they are reflected back to us by those who inhabit our personal sphere, whether they be friend or foe. It is of inestimable value to surround yourself with those whom you can trust to speak the truth.

We find that it is often those situations or persons who appear to create the greatest pain in our lives that are our greatest teachers. The conflict or chaos they ignite within us presents an opportunity to question our perceptions. We then have a choice to remain where we are in the safety of our patterns or to rebalance them, but we cannot stay where we are without prolonging our suffering. Either way, we are called to understand something of our nature.

On another note, the benefits of engaging with a like-minded community are numerous for the developing sensitive. Obviously, a student must rely upon the honesty of a fellow student to be completely forthcoming about any evidence given, in order that the pathways of the mind are laid upon solid foundations. In addition, when like-minded people routinely sit together for the Presence with harmony of intention and for the right reasons, access to the power of the Spirit is augmented over time and the healing potential greatly amplified.

Ego and Oneness

When we speak of the ego in our way, we refer to the self-awareness of being. Ego is neither good nor bad. It just is. As mediums on the pathway to the mystical consciousness, we attempt to expand the awareness of the ego with the intention of making it a more powerful instrument of service to the etheric world and to the Great Spirit.

Egotism, on the other hand, thrives in the illusion that service to self is the end rather than the means. When we feed our vessel with learning for the purposes of self-aggrandizement we have missed the point.

In our way, we regard the ego as something to be spiritually nurtured in the knowledge that it is our only means of being aware of our existence within this existence. We attempt to be self-full in order to be rich in the substance of the God Nature, enhancing our ability to create healing in this world and the next.

Self-full. This is quite a different matter than being selfish. Think of the self as a chalice. When we are not self-full, we drain the chalice. When we fill the chalice until it overflows, we can then be of service in the true nature of our being. At some time or another, we all find ourselves drained, in a state of neediness or of self-loathing. It is only human. But it is our duty, especially as workers for the Spirit, to heal this; to find ways to fill our cup, to be self-full. Only then can we serve another properly. Remember, your nature is your health, your health is your abundance, and your abundance is to be shared in aid of healing humanity. It all begins with your nature.

Naturally, keeping this balance can be a delicate matter and easily upset, particularly in the sensitized field of the intuitive arts. Sadly, we sometimes see jealousy, intolerance or spitefulness rearing its head amongst some practitioners who, in their own neediness, become blind as to why they practise mediumship and who they actually serve.

At birth, we experience the illusion of separation from the Creator in order that, during the course of our lives, we may reacquaint ourselves with the reality of oneness with creation, with the natural world and with self. It is this return journey toward which we all tend, consciously or unconsciously, each in our own manner and each with varying degrees of awareness. Some souls may even choose to increase their experience of separation during their lifetimes for the same purposes as the one who appears to actively seek spiritual unity. All being equal, no path is more or less "spiritual" than another.

Oneness with the Creator is our natural state of being. It is where we came from and where we are now headed. In the interim, in the wisdom of the Infinite Intelligence, an impression of separation from Itself was manifest in the form of ego. The great gift lies in the opportunity it has presented to us, by Grand Design, to do all in our power to close that gap.

We cannot be aware of oneness without having experienced separation. Nor could we be conscious of separation had we not once been one with the Creator. Again, they are two sides of the same coin of divine experience.

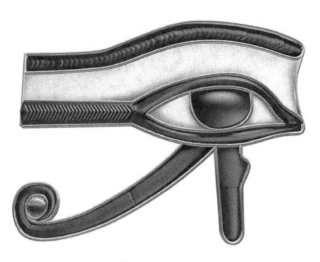

The Eye of Ra

Ra was the sun god, creator of mankind and of all things. The people of Egypt began to disrespect him and Ra was greatly angered at their blasphemy. He sent punishment down upon them in the form of the Eye of Ra, a lion goddess who struck terror into the hearts of the people. Many thousands perished.

Ra saw that the lioness would eventually destroy humanity for, having tasted blood, she would never cease the devastation. So Ra had to trick her. He ordered seven thousand jars of beer coloured with pomegranate juice to be poured over the fields. Thinking it was blood, the lion goddess drank greedily, fell asleep, and thereafter peace reigned once more in Egypt.

Self Control

Chapter Fifteen:
A Questioning Mind

"An age of impulse demands an age of reason."

Andrew Jackson Davis[1]

Common Sense

Embrace your inner sceptic…

If you are an intuitive, whether student or professional, a rational examination of apparent phenomena and psychic events that arise during the course of your development is strongly encouraged. A healthy dose of common sense never goes amiss. Before assuming that an inexplicable occurrence originates within the spirit world, it only makes sense to look at all the possible physical causes.

A blind acceptance of all phenomena, theory and philosophy without an objective, questioning attitude is unwise. We are essentially abdicating responsibility for discernment. At the other extreme, a mind driven by overriding scepticism, fearing to appear foolish, may rob us of the opportunity to *experience* the power of the Presence and its limitless manifestations. Maintaining an intelligent balance of faith and reason is simply common sense.

In intuitive work, we are encouraged to keep scepticism alive in harmonious proportion with an open mind and heart, and to recognise discretion as a positive, useful tool in our spiritual kit. Wisdom lies in finding the proper balance within our practice.

In the stage of magician consciousness, the questioning mind will and should be asking, "How much of this information is my own perception and how much is the etheric world? To what degree am I overlaying my interpretation on this reading? Where is this information really coming from?" The recipient of any message or phenomenon should be equally astute. Be awake to the quality of evidence the medium gives you.

What we are ideally looking for is a healthy sceptical mind that is able to evaluate with equanimity. It is a wise practitioner who can look with detachment at phenomena and received impressions with a mindset which is neither wishful nor judgmental.

The next step is to quieten the chatter that tells us that our intuition is not real, and to allow the psychic or mediumistic experience to unfold in the present moment. We mustn't allow scepticism to rob us of a spiritual experience. We want to acknowledge the experience and accord it its rightful place. To do otherwise would be to disrespect those who wish to communicate with us.

A questioning mind, well employed, will lead us to a sureness about our beliefs, and a confidence in the evidence we offer. Because we have allowed ourselves to question and to arrive at our own conclusions based on personal experience of communication with the etheric world, we can move forward confidently in the knowledge of our ability, and be of even greater service to humanity.

In the depth of our understanding of the power of the Spirit, we then open our hearts and minds to make way for the, as yet, unimaginable manifestations of the Spirit in our world.

Daedalus and Icarus

There once lived a great architect called Daedalus. King Minos commissioned Daedalus to build a labyrinth to imprison the monster, Minotaur, whom the King kept to kill his enemies. Daedalus built a maze so clever that escape was impossible and the king was well pleased.

When the king's daughter, Ariadne, fell in love with Theseus, who came to slay the Minotaur, Daedalus gave him a ball of thread so that, unravelling it as he went, he could then find his way out. King Minos was furious at this betrayal and imprisoned Daedalus and his son, Icarus, in the labyrinth. So Daedalus created gigantic wings of feathers and wax and, making their escape, he warned his son not to fly too close to the sun or the wings would melt. But Icarus, drunk with the adoration of those who saw him fly and thought him a god, flew too close to the sun and fell into the sea.

Humility

Chapter Sixteen: Word to the Wise

"Think purely, speak truly, love nobly."

H.D. Barrett[1]

Ethical Practice

A little bit of knowledge is dangerous.

The concepts and ideas shared in this volume are but part of a vast whole, an ocean of philosophical understanding from which no single element can be utilised in isolation without it becoming potentially injurious to the psyche of the practitioner and to those within his or her sphere of influence.

The ethical practice of transcommunication is motivated by the desire to serve and to serve well. It is inspired by the knowledge that Spirit, or the Infinite Intelligence known as God, is the source of all power, healing and manifestation.

Therefore, the fullest possible understanding of this ancient knowledge, and the proper use of these principles, is our spiritual and moral responsibility. It takes discipline. It takes training. It takes work.

For the spiritual ramifications are beyond imagining.

In Pursuit of Awakening

If you possess intuitive, psychic or mediumistic skills, it is because you were born with an ability. It has everything to do with genetic makeup and intrinsically little to do with spiritual awareness. In other words, just because someone is a medium doesn't automatically make them more or less spiritually enlightened than someone who is not.

The truly great gift of possessing the mediumistic ability is not only the ability itself but the privilege it affords us as a means of personal transformation. This is one of the reasons we have *any* of the talents we do. As we hone them, use them, challenge them and allow them to open our inner eyes, so do we allow them to transform us in our humanity and our spirituality, for there is no separation.

In the esoteric tradition in which we work, one of our core intentions as mystics is that of fulfilling our soul's purpose toward enlightenment. Today, we often see methods of psychic training along purely technical lines with little grasp of spiritual foundations. This could be likened to forever sharpening your cooking utensils but never using them to prepare a meal.

When you engage your ability in the pursuit of awakening your own spirit; when you embody the highest standards of integrity in order to serve the needs of those spirits, both seen and unseen, who cross your path, then you become awake to the spiritual magnitude of your chosen way as intuitives, psychics and mediums.

How do we begin? Heal ourselves. It all begins with us. As we heal, so do we heal others. It cannot be otherwise. For as the great Lao Tzu says, "He who knows others is wise; he who knows himself is enlightened."[2]

It is surely no accident that you are reading this book. Those who earnestly search for a deeper significance will be guided along the right path for their soul's progression. For some, not all, the mediumistic way to spiritual unfoldment may be that path.

Laying Down Pathways of Discovery

We, as teachers, are attempting to lead you to the discovery of the process of your own ability, to guide you in laying down pathways of the mind as opposed to "getting it right." Imagine that you are walking through a field of new grass where no one has walked before. Every time you walk down the path you have created, you open it out, smooth it out, perceive more around you, and become familiar with the experience. So it is with the development of the intuitive's mind.

Good training, frank feedback, patience, perseverance, practice and enjoyment will allow your ability to develop naturally and ethically.

At this point, we feel it our duty to remind those mediums and students of mediumship who may be grieving, to lay aside their practice for a time. Continuing to develop during this period puts you at considerable risk for augmenting mental distress and may put undue strain upon your ability.

Knowledge and Knowing

Knowledge is good. As mediums, we need to understand what we do, how we do it and, most importantly, why we do it. Use the mind to reason, to inquire, to discern. Let knowledge be the foundation of your art.

Knowing, on the other hand, comes about through experience. It has little to do with reason, but is rather an understanding of the soul.

Knowledge will not bring us knowing. Knowledge simply allows us to understand the experience.

Attitude

The intuitive arts are not competitive. There is no ultimate external goal to achieve, nor should you ever compare yourself with another. The need to do so will only inhibit your ability.

Everyone works differently, receives differently, and perceives differently. It is your job to come to know how that looks and feels. What words, symbols, images, sensations make up your vocabulary of psychic language? They will not be the same as anyone else's. Do not compare yourself with others at any stage in your development. Such comparisons create stumbling blocks for you and, further down the road, may well diminish your natural ability.

Simply be in the fullness of who you are and allow that honest light to be.

Developing Naturally with Gratitude

Find out where your natural abilities lie. In our eagerness and anxiety to know more and to develop our ability too quickly, we often try too hard. Grabbing desperately at techniques which don't present themselves spontaneously or naturally, and forcing a desired result without first understanding its nature, will ultimately have the opposite of the desired outcome.

Relax. Find out where your natural abilities flow and leave the rest to emerge in its time. In this way, you will develop your abilities in the correct *harmonious* proportion. The development of your psychism and mediumship cannot be rushed.

You want to gently stretch your mind in development, not break it! Don't lie to yourself about your ability. You will only succeed in dampening it down. So be honest about it. Instead, work with your natural tendencies as a starting point. Always be in gratitude for the talents you possess, the opportunities and awarenesses that you presently have, and take pleasure in the process. Let your ability shine.

The Ego

In our understanding, ego is necessary for survival. It is part of our instinctive nature. Ego is simply self-concern and is actually essential to our physical survival as a species.

Within our practice of transcommunication, we do not try to suppress the ego as is demanded by some disciplines. Rather, we encourage an unblinking view of it, honestly acknowledging its attributes whether they be welcome or unwelcome, and creating a balance so that we can work with it instead of against it. It has much to teach us.

For it is through the ego's experience, both its shadows and its light, that we seek to become the best human being we can be and move with spiritual integrity toward that oneness with the Divine. This approach, however, requires much more of us than does simple suppression of the ego's less desirable aspects. It asks for complete transparency in our dealings with self. It is hard work with great rewards.

Egotism is another matter. Acts of egotism are a sign that the individual's shadow has overpowered his or her light, and that equilibrium has been lost, hopefully only temporarily.

We must be ever vigilant in matters pertaining to our ego, which may seek to grab the spotlight. A medium who manoeuvres to make a piece of evidence fit is attempting to rescue his or her ego rather than serve the needs of the loved one in the afterlife.

Therefore, it is our duty to leave the ego's neediness at the door every time our service as a medium is required.

Once again, we must take personal responsibility for our actions, and do so in the sure knowledge that those we represent in the etheric world will either be in our debt or be our debtors. We shall be held accountable. Nothing and no one escapes the divine laws of compensation. Truth is the environment in which we all must work.

A Cautionary Note

A psychic or medium is neither a counsellor nor a diagnostician. Our job is not to advise or fix but rather to provide the environment for transformation. The practice of psychology and medical diagnostics by an untrained practitioner is not only dangerous but illegal without proper certification.

The Two Jackals

There were once two jackals who lived in the desert and were devoted friends. They ate, drank and hunted together, and always shared the same patch of shade.

One day as they rested beneath the branches of a desert tree, they saw a ferocious lion bounding towards them, intent on a good meal. The two jackals stood quite still until the lion reached them. The lion was puzzled by this and roared out, "Are your limbs stiff with age? Didn't you see me coming? Why haven't you run away?"

"Lord Lion," answered the jackals, "we saw you coming in your fury and we decided not to run. You would have overtaken us anyway, and why should we tire ourselves out before we are eaten?"

The lion was amused by this answer and let the two jackals go.

Acceptance

Chapter Seventeen:
Dialogues

*"Knowledge and wisdom are priceless assets.
The first has to be acquired and the second cultivated."*

Arthur Findlay[1]

How does sitting for the presence of the Spirit differ from meditation?

It is important to understand that these two practices are completely different. Though they may appear to be similar, they are opposing mental processes.

Meditation is a valuable tool for developing concentration and relaxing the mind. There is a conscious withdrawal into the inner psyche and the goal is to arrive at a calm, restful state of mind. When sitting in the Presence, we are setting aside the mundane activities of the mind and opening the whole vessel of self to allow for the presence of the Spirit. We are practising the art of listening. It is a state of alertness and, in that sense, active.

Let us remember that you cannot be where God is not. Sitting for the Presence is simply applying our focus in such a way as to heighten our *awareness* of the Power. The deliberate practice of sitting for the Presence is actually a relatively recent construct, made necessary by the distractions of our modern world.

Meditation is self-focused. Sitting in the Presence is God-focused. Energetically speaking, the two practices are poles apart. Therefore, if you are a developing intuitive, it is not recommended that you combine these two practices. Either sit or meditate, but not in the same session or with the same intention.

What is the difference between a sitting and a reading?

A sitting is a private appointment with a medium primarily for the purpose of contacting the discarnate being. The older word, séance, is a gathering or "circle" of those who sit for the presence of the Spirit and comes from the Latin "sedere" meaning "sit".

During a private or public reading, the practitioner works on a psychic level to gather information from the aura of the incarnate recipient.

If, during a public demonstration of mediumship, the medium is giving more information about the recipient than about the spirit contact, it is usually a fairly clear indication that the demonstrator has switched from mediumship to psychism. It is paramount that a practitioner knows the difference and does not try to pass off one for the other. Each method is extremely valuable in its rightful place, but we must call a spade a spade. Again, we are ethically responsible and spiritually accountable.

When attending a demonstration or going for a private appointment, it must also be said that the best results will ensue if the recipient is both open-minded and discerning, receptive as well as alert. Under these relaxed and hopeful conditions, the intuitive will be able to offer his or her best work.

How do I know if a medium is authentic?

When we are grieving or emotionally vulnerable, the heart wrenching desire to hear just one more word from a loved one is overwhelming and can naturally cloud our rational judgment. It is a sad fact that the profession of mediumship has long been tainted by some who have taken advantage of the vulnerable in the most immoral way. As a consequence, it has been an ongoing struggle to continually reaffirm the innate integrity and sacredness of this noble art form.

A basic rule of thumb in assessing the work of a medium is to look for verification through evidence. It is not enough that a medium pronounces, "I have your father here," and immediately proceeds to wax poetic with a message. We must expect some recognisable evidence of survival. The discerning recipient should expect verification to confirm that a contact has actually been made.

These evidential details might include names and dates, favourite pastimes, likes and dislikes, profession, country of residence, shared memories, relationships, nicknames, manner of passing and other relevant details. One of the most pivotal types of verification occurs when a medium gives the recipient evidence of which the recipient is unaware at the time and which is later discovered to be correct.

When a grieving soul receives a message of love and recognition from their loved one in the etheric world, a profound healing can take place in both worlds. This is one of the most valuable healing services a medium can offer to both those in the etheric world and the bereaved here on the earth.

Has the spirit of my departed loved one arrived safely in the spirit world?

For those who grieve the death of a loved one, this is often the first question that arises. We take the utmost care to make ourselves clearly understood on this sensitive point.

The answer is always, "Yes."

The natural laws of the Great Spirit do not include judgment by a vengeful figurehead bent on punishment. The universe and all things in it are governed by natural law including the event called death. It is impossible to interfere with our transition from this world to the next, no matter how death occurs. This is a fabrication of fear and, despite the astonishing endurance of such notions, they have no truth or bearing in spiritual reality.

When someone dies, ties with this physical sphere are loosened and the soul of the individual immediately begins the transformative journey into the etheric world, often aided by friends and family who have gone before. There are no stops along the way and no traps set for bad behaviour. At the very least, common sense must surely prevail on this point.

Would you talk about haunting and spirit rescue?

There is a great deal of misunderstanding around so-called "haunting." Television programs claiming to investigate haunted houses and accomplish dramatic spirit rescues shamelessly capitalise upon the fear of the unknown and, while such episodes are highly inventive, they have very little to do with reality. Unfortunately, one must likewise be wary of those who prey upon the innocent, offering, for instance, to rid one's house of an evil spirit, generally for a hefty fee.

The real explanation for so-called hauntings may be somewhat less sensational but is far more fascinating because it is true, and because it exemplifies yet another wondrous natural law.

Every location, every living being, every object has a core energy. Superimposed upon this core energy are layers of mental, physical and emotional energy accumulated over time from earthly experiences, events, collective attitudes and repetitive actions.

A building, for example, may accumulate layers of energy based on repeated incidents that have taken place within its walls. Whenever an activity is re-enacted, its energy is amplified and, over time, accumulates. When the activity ceases, this energetic memory naturally begins to fade.

However, when a sensitive individual enters that venue, they may receive impressions regarding the nature of past events and the people involved. This information is received psychically from the residual energy of dramatic positive or negative events that have occurred at that location and that are present still within its energetic memory. It may also happen that an untrained individual with latent psychic tendencies could unwittingly reignite this energy and cause certain phenomena to reactivate.

If the professional sensitive understands these facts and is properly trained, he or she may work to release or transform the unwanted residual energy within that location. But as there is no discarnate presence in this case, there is no mediumistic involvement. There is no such thing as a spirit "trapped" between worlds and therefore never any unfortunate soul that needs rescuing. To suggest otherwise would be to imply that the Creator has lost control of creation. The God Mind and the natural laws of the universe simply do not work in this way.

Is my personality the same as my soul?

Many confuse personality with soul. Your personality is the cloak your soul wears throughout your life on earth, the threads of which are created by genetic makeup, biology, environment, circumstances, choices and experience.

Personality is a composite mask reflecting the character which we have created throughout our lives. The mask of personality has been moulded largely from the clay of experience and culminates in certain attitudes, perceptions, actions and reactions to the environment in which the soul finds itself.

Personality is but one of the soul's many aspects, identifiable characteristics that make up the garment which the soul wears during its passage on earth.

What is the difference between soul and spirit?

Your body, mind and emotions are expressions of the soul.

Your soul is the expression of your spirit.

Your spirit is the expression of the Great Spirit.

Your soul is the godchild of your spirit. Soul is not immortal. Your spirit is immortal, being a facet of the Great Spirit, which is eternal.

Your soul encompasses aspects of your personality with its challenges and strengths; it encompasses aspects of your mind and thought patterns, aspects of your emotional makeup, and of your spiritual nature. It gives identity to the "you" and animates your life on earth.

Your spirit describes that essence of you which is a spark of the Divine Nature, and which is eternal. The spirit animates the soul. Someone once expressed it in this very down-to-earth way, "Your immortal spirit is that part of you which you cannot imagine dead."

And, in fact, once the body, mind, emotions and soul manifestations have completed their tasks, the spirit will return to blend with the Source. The essence that is the real you will continue and by that essence will you be known. We do not automatically become "new and improved" upon passing to etherea. As one of our ancestors, Emanuel Swedenborg, once said, "In the spiritual body moreover, man appears such as he is with respect to love and faith, for everyone in the spiritual world is the effigy of his own love...."[2]

Raven Steals the Sun

There was once a chief who coveted all things so much so that he stole the sun and placed it in a box in front of his longhouse. The world was plunged into darkness and suffering.

The Raven, who had existed from the beginning of time, wearied of the darkness and transformed himself into a beautiful man-child. He visited the chief and immediately captivated him with his wisdom and beauty. The chief showered Raven with many gifts. However, he was told that under no circumstances was he to touch the box containing the sun.

Time went on and still the chief refused to open the box. However, Raven was patient and persistent and constantly flattered the chief until one day he finally gave in to Raven's request to show him the contents of the box. Immediately Raven transformed back into himself, caught the sun in his beak and placed the golden orb back in the heavens.

Light returned to the world and humankind's suffering ended.

Awakening

Chapter Eighteen:
A Parting Thought

Make Life Beautiful

"Let us do what we can, every one.
If we cannot do great things, as they are outwardly measured and weighed,
we can each one of us do something. If every life cannot be conspicuous –
which is not what it is for –
it can at least be beautiful…

We need not think it necessary to work for the applause or praise of men.
It is well for us to keep in mind that it is not we who do these worthy deeds,
but the spirit within that is continually inspiring."

Anonymous[1]

A Sacred Art

The medium and the mystic find themselves at the hub of three states of consciousness – the upper realms of spirit, the inner realm of the psyche and the outer realm of material illusion.

In our philosophy, we understand that our job is to recognise our personal patterns and heal our sometimes conflicted relationship with the outer world in order to bring about peace in our inner world. Naturally, this is a desirable goal for any human being but for the mystic it is essential. When our personal filters and judgments are active, how can we possibly hope to perceive what really *is*? We would basically be looking through a prism.

Healing ourselves does not mean suppression of all the dark, unappealing sides of our makeup. Healing ourselves means accepting our humanity, recognising our triggers, calming our personal demons and amplifying our talents. In short, returning to our true nature.

As we move closer to what we call our Beauty, our inner clarity expands and we become more fitting channels for service to the upper realms. We detach from our own perceptions. We come to see the reality of things and communicate these without judgment.

There is an iconic image of the Lion consuming the Sun, the Lion being the outer realm and the Sun being your ability. In the world of mediumship, we regrettably find those whose need for feeding from the outer world and for public acclaim overrides the intention of service to the etheric world. During a public demonstration, for instance, some mediums may resort to a psychic reading of the aura while keeping up a semblance of spirit communication. To be perfectly clear, there is nothing amiss with either method. It is the dishonesty or ignorance that damages. The medium has been pulled into the outer world and has lost touch with the inner and upper awareness. Just as the Lion consumes the Sun, so the light of our ability may be consumed. Our soul cannot long be sustained by the illusion.

The ability to stand in your truth, to hold your space and be in your Beauty is a practice not just for an hour's passage on the platform of a public arena, but for a lifetime. These precepts are constantly in the awareness of those who seek the consciousness of the mystic, and emanation of the healing influences of the Presence will accompany such a person wherever they may go.

So feed your own spirit with the things of the Spirit. Allow your talents to shine. Stand in your Beauty. Be self-full. Heal. Sit. Be in the Presence. Know when to work and when not to work. Use your ability in complete honesty. Awaken to your moral and ethical truth. Your eternity depends upon it.

The mission of the mystic has always been to reveal the reality of the Creator's creation in all its wonder to those prepared to reverently see it. Transcommunication in the old way was but one aspect of this mission, one of the many ways of revealing the hidden mysteries.

Mysticism is not found in a demonstration of platform mediumship. It was never meant to be the message-driven spectacle which is sometimes prevalent today. Mysticism was a sacred art practised by those who understood the nature of the Divine and who, in reverent harmony with the God Nature, had mastered the hard-won disciplines necessary to become the instruments of revelation.

Only those still working within the magician consciousness would call themselves mystics. The true mystic, on the other hand, under-stands that he or she is always and ever a student. The life of the mystic is a life of dedication, discipline and service whose purpose it is to create unity; the unity which encompasses all within the One. For by returning to the One, we can then give to the many.

Those of our lineage who work in this way "know" each other. There are signs and symbols which telegraph our recognition of another who is of our tradition. For those who may resonate with our way and seek to be trained within it, may we caution you that not every teacher who speaks our words actually understands our language.

In our way of developing the whole and balanced medium and mystic, our intention has ever been to reawaken the sacred mysteries so that they become fully woven into the fabric of transcommunica-tion. Needless to say, it requires a somewhat greater commitment on the part of the developing medium or mystic than is normally asked for in a weekend workshop. It is not for everyone.

It is our hope that, with these broad spiritual foundations, the world may be touched by the work of those capable of bringing about a healing, not only to an individual, but to the consciousness of the human race. Peace is most earnestly to be wished for.

~

Brian Robertson
and
Simon James

As above, so below. As within, so without.
As without, so within. As below, so above.

As the One touches your spirit, so may you touch the outer world.
This is the great privilege of your talent.
Use it wisely.

"The true mystic is a man who enters into
full possession of his inner life."

HYMNS OF HERMES

Vocatus Atque Non Vocatus, Deus Aderit.

.

About the Authors

About Brian Robertson

Brian Robertson is an internationally known medium, spiritual lecturer and highly respected teacher of transcommunication. He is founder and president of the Inner Quest, a centre of study for the ethical development of mediums and serious students of the intuitive arts. He teaches at major colleges and institutions around the world, and is a much sought-after advisor to multi-faith religious organisations, sharing the breadth of his esoteric knowledge both as a keynote speaker on international platforms and in documentary film, radio and television.

Brian Robertson's distinguished career has been devoted to re-establishing a sacred vitality within esoteric mediumship and its associated arts, and to the development of ethical practitioners who understand that, without spiritual awareness, we leave but a poor legacy to the world. His down-to-earth guidance demands not only our attention, but our participation, encouraging us to unfold the spirit within each one of us and thereby create the beauty we wish to see in the world.

About Simon James

Simon James is one of today's finest classical spiritual mediums and a living link to the British tradition of the early 20th century, having been one of only five mediums chosen to be personally trained by the renowned Gordon Higginson. He is a director of the Inner Quest in Canada and teaches at major centres in Australia, Great Britain, the United States, Europe and around the world. Simon James holds a degree in Applied Psychology and has extensive knowledge of mythology, the tarot and related disciplines which inform his work with mediums, teachers and medical professionals worldwide.

Simon James is above all a healer and a Renaissance man, whose depth of knowledge of mythology, ancient religion, and esoteric tradition underlies the richness of his teaching in the classroom, on international podiums and in the media. His humour and depth of compassion uplift all who come within his compass the world over, as he shares his innate wisdom as teacher, guide, inspirational speaker and world renowned spiritual medium.

About the Inner Quest

The Inner Quest is devoted to the ethical and esoteric development of those pursuing the intuitive arts. Its purpose is to facilitate an awareness of our natural spiritual foundations within the practices of healing mediumship, personal transformation and many of the lesser known aspects of the esoteric experience.

The Inner Quest also provides an ongoing program of classical study for the serious student and is host to several international retreats. The Inner Quest has established a worldwide reputation for developing sound spiritual practitioners, fostering creativity within our "everyday mediumship", and reigniting the intrinsically sacred nature of the intuitive arts. It also houses the Inner Quest Press which has published this and other books.

The Inner Quest is based in Victoria, Canada. Founders Brian Robertson and Simon James have long been sharing their unique esoteric knowledge at major venues around the world by means of public demonstrations, private consultations, television, film, lectures and courses. Within every facet of their extensive practice is to be found a profound dedication to serve all who seek a path to spiritual unfoldment.

We invite you to discover more about the Inner Quest by visiting our website.

Inner Quest Foundation

A Glossary of Terms

It may be useful to those beginning to work with their sensitivity to have a basic understanding of how we in our tradition use certain terms within the context of the intuitive arts. These may or may not precisely correspond to the dictionary definition, but are meant as a common point of reference for those involved in the fields of psychism and transcommunication.

Apport and Asport: The relocation of an object from one place to another, or the appearance of an object from an unknown location without apparent or visible means.

Attunement: The act of moving one's mind to a state in which one blends with the Presence for the purposes of healing and transcommunication.

Aura: Subtle fields of energy emanating from a person or object, reflecting who and what we are physically, mentally, and emotionally.

Beauty: Your nature, your truth and your light as you were created within soul formation.

Consciousness: The quality of being aware of the mind itself.

Discarnate: Being without a physical body.

Energy: An aspect of force inherent within all beings and objects which can be transformed but never destroyed. Energy belongs to the material realm even though it is invisible. It varies in intensity depending upon time, circumstance, location and the ability of the medium to amplify its effects, which are finite.

Esoteric: From the Greek, "inner." Esoteric knowledge implies mystical knowledge of the inner realms that are hidden from view.

Etheric: Of the ether. The spiritual energy within creation; that substance which interpenetrates all things. Refers also to the many worlds including that most commonly referred to as the spirit world or afterlife.

Incarnate: Being within a physical body.

Magician: A formative stage of awareness in which the student views outer phenomena as the goal in and of itself as opposed to a step along the pathway toward mediumistic and mystic consciousness.

Manifestation: The material embodiment of an unseen force. Manifestations may include healing, communication, apports and asports, inspirational writing, precipitated art and other forms of psychic phenomena.

Mechanics: Techniques and methods used by intuitive practitioners to develop their ability to receive information from incarnate and discarnate sources. Mechanical mediumship refers to the use of these techniques without acknowledgement of their spiritual implications.

Mediumship: The healing practice of communion and communication with what is known as the etheric world.

Mysticism: Inner spiritual disciplines which reveal knowledge of divine law for the purpose of unity with the God Mind.

Perception: The filters through which each person assesses self, others and the world.

Power: The underlying Intelligent Force that permeates all things, seen and unseen. The God-power is eternal, constant and unaffected by time, space or circumstance. It is ever present and infinite. The Power is God.

Precognition: From the Latin, "before" + "knowing." A foreknowledge that a particular and specific set of circumstances could potentially take place; an accurate impression of a future event.

Premonition: From the Latin, "before" + "warn." A sense that something is about to happen. Usually, the information is felt and the anticipated circumstances are undefined.

Psychism: The act of receiving information from an incarnate source by means of auric vibration.

Psychokinesis: From the Greek, "mind" + "movement." The ability to effect movement of objects in the material world by means of mental energy.

Psychometry: From the Greek, "soul" + "measurement." The ability to obtain information about the history and nature of an object or an individual by psychic means.

Signature: A recognisable aspect of the blueprint of the soul. Signature refers to the unique character and nature of the emanation created by an individual or group.

Soul: The individualised aspect of Spirit. Spirit animates soul which in turn animates our earthly vessel.

Spirit: The Divine Presence we may call God.

Spiritualism: In its original intention, a religious philosophy which acknowledges the Divine Intelligence in all things, embraces mediumistic disciplines within its practice, acknowledges the continuity of life, encourages personal responsibility, and recognises that the primary purpose of mediumship is that of healing.

Synchronicity: Term coined by Carl Jung, in conjunction with W. Pauli, to describe a simultaneous occurrence of events that appear significantly related but have no apparent causal connection.

Theurgy: From the Greek "theourgia": the quest for union with, and the manifestation of, the Divine.

Trance: An altered state of consciousness.

Trance Impersonation: An altered state of consciousness in which the identifiable voice of a known personality manifests and speaks directly to a sitter.

Transcommunication: Communication between the seen and unseen worlds, including the faculty commonly referred to as mediumship.

Triad: A three-fold philosophical contemplation; a trio of related ideas which encourage our participation in the unfoldment of our spiritual humanity.

Vibration: Patterns of energy derived from matter or spirit.

List of Illustrations

References

Introduction

1. Heraclitus, c.500 BC.
2. Campbell, Joseph. 1988. *The Power of Myth*. Anchor Books, USA.

Chapter 1: A Message from Simon and Brian

1. Schuré, Edouard. 1910. From the introduction to *The Way of Initiation by R. Steiner*. Macoy Publishing Company, Richmond, VA, USA.

Chapter 2: Magician to Mystic

1. Porphyry. c.270 AD. *The Life of Plotinus*.
2. Mead, G.R.S. 1906. *Echoes from the Gnosis*. The Gnostic Society Library, CA.
3. Yoganada, Paramhansa. 1946. *Autobiography of a Yogi*. The Philosophical Library, New York, NY.

Chapter 4: Alchemy of the Soul

1. Schlesinger, Julia. 1896. *Workers in the Vineyard*. San Francisco, CA.
2. Davis, Andrew Jackson. 1852. *The Great Harmonia*. Benjamin B. Massey & Company, Boston, MA.
3. Mead, G.R.S. 1906. *Echoes from the Gnosis*. The Gnostic Society Library, CA.
4. Davis, Andrew Jackson. 1852. *The Great Harmonia*. Benjamin B. Massey & Company, Boston, MA.

Chapter 5: Spirituality and Mediumship

1. Morse, J.J. 1888. *Practical Occultism*. Carrier Dove Publishing House, San Francisco, CA.

Chapter 6: Nature of the Intuitive Arts

1. Watson, Elizabeth Lowe. 1905. *Song and Sermon*. Hicks-Judd Company, San Francisco, CA.
2. Schlesinger, Julia. 1896. *Workers in the Vineyard*. San Francisco, CA.
3. Yogananda, Paramhansa. 1946. *Autobiography of a Yogi*. The Philosophical Library, New York, NY.
4. Hardinge Britten, Emma. 1860. *Six Lectures on Theology and Nature*. Published by the Author.

Chapter 7: Quality of Discernment

1. Swedenborg, Emmanuel. 1763. *Divinity and Space*. Sapientia Angelica de Divino Amore. Amsterdam, Holland.
2. Porphyry. c.270 AD. *The Life of Plotinus*.
3. Andersen, H.C. (1837). "The Emperor's New Clothes", originally published in Eventyr, fortalte for Børn (*Fairy Tales, Told for Children*), Denmark.
4. Azur the Helper in *Precipitated Spirit Paintings* by Ron Nagy. Lily Dale, NY.

Chapter 8: Becoming a Balanced Medium

1. Davis, Andrew Jackson. 1868. *Answers to Ever-recurring Questions from the People: A Sequel to the Penetralia*. William White & Company, Boston, MA.
2. Steiner, Rudolf. 1910. *The Way of Initiation*. Macoy Publishing Company, Richmond, VA.
3. Brother Lawrence. c.1650. *The Practice of the Presence of God*. Public domain.

Chapter 9: Toward Your Beauty

1. Bailey, Philip James. 1839. *Festus*. Public domain.
2. Davis, Andrew Jackson. 1852. *The Great Harmonia*. Benjamin B. Massey & Company, Boston, MA.
3. Porphyry. c.270 AD. *The Life of Plotinus*.
4. Aristotle. c.350 BC.

Chapter 10: The Triads

1. Swedenborg, Emmanuel. 1763. *Divinity and Space*. Sapientia Angelica de Divino Amore. Amsterdam, Holland.
2. Pythagoras. c.530 BC.

Chapter 11: Voice of the Soul

1. Higginson, Gordon. 1993. *On the Side of Angels*. Compiled by Jean Bassett. SNU Publications, Stansted, Essex, UK.
2. Transire as defined in the Oxford English Dictionary.
3. Pope, Alexander. 1732. *Essay on Man*.
4. Higginson, Gordon. 1993. *On the Side of Angels*. Compiled by Jean Bassett. SNU Publications, Stansted, Essex, UK.
5. Magritte, René. Common quotation.

Chapter 12: To Heal

1. Johanson, Tom. 1986. *First Heal the Mind*. Bishopsgate Press, London, UK.

Chapter 13: Death

1. Hugo, Victor. 1802-1885. Common quotation.
2. Tzu, Lao. 6th –5th century BC. *Tao Te Ching*.

Chapter 14: For Your Contemplation

1. Davis, Andrew Jackson. 1852. *The Great Harmonia*. Benjamin B. Massey & Company, Boston, MA.
2. Pythagoras. c.530 BC.

Chapter 15: A Questioning Mind

1. Davis, Andrew Jackson. 1852. *The Great Harmonia*. Benjamin B. Massey & Company, Boston, MA.

Chapter 16: Word to the Wise

1. Barrett, H. D. c.1898. Excerpt from *Banner of Light*. Boston, MA.
2. Tzu, Lao. 6th –5th century BC. *Tao Te Ching*.

Chapter 17: Dialogues

1. Findlay, Arthur. 1948. *The Curse of Ignorance*. Psychic Press Ltd., UK.
2. Swedenborg, Emmanuel. 1763. *Divinity and Space*. Sapientia Angelica de Divino Amore. Amsterdam, Holland.

Chapter 18: A Parting Thought

1. Anonymous. 1871. *The Medium and Daybreak*, London, UK.

Milton Keynes UK
Ingram Content Group UK Ltd.
UKHW031119120824
1228UKWH00020B/247